The Art of Poetry volume 14

Cambridge IGCSE, Songs of Ourselves

Published by Peripeteia Press Ltd.

First published June 2017

ISBN: 978-1-9997376-0-3

Peripeteia.webs.com

Contents

General Introduction to the The Art of Poetry series

The philosopher Nietzsche described his work as 'the greatest gift that [mankind] has ever been given'. The Elizabethan poet Edmund Spenser hoped his epic, *The Faerie Queene,* would magically transform its readers into noblemen. In comparison, our aims for *The Art of Poetry* series of books are a little more modest. Fundamentally we aim to provide books that will be of maximum use to English students and their teachers. In our experience, few students read essays on poems, yet, whatever specification they are studying, they have to write analytical essays on poetry. So, we've offering some models, written in a lively, accessible and, we hope, engaging style. We believe that the essay as a form needs demonstrating and championing, especially as so many revision books for students present information in broken down note form.

For Volume 1 we chose canonical poems for several reasons: Firstly, they are simply great poems, well worth reading and studying; secondly, we chose poems from across time so that they sketch in outline major developments in English poetry, from the Elizabethan period up until the present day, so that the volume works as an introduction to poetry and poetry criticism. Our popular volumes 2-5 focused on poems set at A-level by the Edexcel and AQA boards respectively. Volumes 6 to 11 tackled GCSE anthologies from AQA, Eduqas, OCR and Edexcel's. In this current volume, we our focus turns to IGCSE, providing critical support for students reading poems about from Cambridge's IGCSE poetry anthology. In particular, we hope our book will inspire those students aiming to reach the very highest grades.

1

Introduction to Volume 14, *Songs of Ourselves*

Like every other GCSE examination board, CIE are looking for perceptive reading, sophisticated understanding and precise analysis of language and of poetic devices. In examiners' speak you have to demonstrate 'critical understanding', 'respond sensitively and in detail to the way the writer achieve his/her effects' and you have to 'integrate much well-selected reference to the text' into your answer. For the highest grade, A* in old money, 9 in the new numerical grading system, you also have to do all this, like Heidi and her blue hair, i.e. with a touch of 'individuality and flair'. One way of learning how to demonstrate that individuality and flair is to follow the advice set out in this book. We put a premium on responses to the poems that do not follow a pre-set agenda or essay recipe and we think your writing should express your own thoughts and feelings informed by your teachers, your peers and your wider reading. And we believe your critical understanding should be expressed in your own emerging critical voice. Hopefully reading our essays will also help too. But to hit the very top, you'll need to supplement what we have written in our essays with your own observations about the poems. The whole of your essay doesn't need to be original and you don't need to complete reinvent the essay form, but a little originality goes along way, in life, in art and in Literature exams.

Unlike other examination boards, CIE puts a premium on your own response to the poems. Their list of adjectives describing top level performance is: 'perceptive, convincing and relevant'. The last of these doesn't sound too demanding, except that it qualifies 'personal' - a 'relevant, personal response'. Now, ideally what CIE are after is what we have just described - an essay that conveys your own thoughts, informed by others, expressed in your own critical voice. What they absolutely do not want is the mere repetition of a model essay that has been provided by a secondary source, whether this source is a teacher, the internet or even a book like this. Nor do they want from a school's GCSE cohort identikit essays all following exactly the same structure, all using the same evidence with the same analysis, all expressing the same ideas and second-hand opinions with varying degrees of confidence.

When you are developing knowledge and understanding of these poems and of how to write successful Literature essays it can be very helpful to use writing frames.

And, of course, it is also fine if the bulk of your essay communicates the analysis you, your class and/or your teacher have developed on the poems, or, indeed you pick up from reading our essays. But like a child learning to ride a bike, if you want to reach the top grades, at some point you need to dispense with the stabilisers and go it alone. If your teacher always insists you follow a writing framework, try to provide original analysis within this. Or, if you're feeling bolder, delight your teacher by breaking out of the frame and producing something more individual and original. Just make sure that the content is very good and that the frame is robust.

If you develop your own appreciation, if you write essays that genuinely express your own, informed thinking and you do this well, you will reach a top grade. In an ideal world everyone in your class would produce different responses, because we are all different and have different tastes, preferences, life experiences and so forth. However, it's also helpful to realistic about this and to have a few tricks up your sleeve, just to make sure the CIE examiners credit you fully for the personal element of your response. It's worth bearing in mind that automatically you will not reach A*, or 9, unless  there is clear evidence of this personal dimension to your essay. And also remember that it is only on the poetry essay that you have to demonstrate this.

So, our advice is that in your poetry essay you draw explicit attention to yourself as a reader at least a few times, perhaps three times over the course of your essay. Generally using the first person singular 'I' is considered naive style in academic literary essays, so we recommend instead you the phrases 'for me' and 'in my opinion'. Clearly there's little point in employing these phrases before factual information. Writing 'for me Tennyson's poem is called *Tears, Idle, Tears* would obviously be stupid. So reserve these phrases for when you are evaluating the effectiveness of a device or feature, as in, 'for me the most powerful way in which Mew expresses her distress is through the form of her poem'. Now that is an opinion, one that you're going to have to use evidence, and use it well, to persuade someone else to accept. These personalising phrases can also usefully be employed in your conclusion to provide a final, distinctively individual angle on the poem and the essay title.

The examination

In the Literature exam. you will have to write one poetry essay. You will be given a choice of two questions on the poems from the *Songs of Ourselves* poetry anthology. Both questions will name specific poems and will include a printed copy of them. Mostly CIE exam questions ask you to respond to one specific poem and they tend to phrase their questions in the 'how does the writer' style. This should focus your attention on the key aspects of what the writers have to say about the topic of the poem and what methods they use to explore this topic. Occasionally, CIE set a question with two short poems. It's important to know that in the exam, if you choose to write on two poems that there are no marks set aside for comparison. You can, in fact, write about the poems separately and still achieve full marks. Hence, this seems to be a more difficult task and we'd generally recommend that you don't choose.

In their examination reports CIE often comment on the fact that many pupils ignore the little, but essential, word 'how' which should focus your attention on writers' methods. And here are a few more useful words of wisdom from the chief examiner's report:

'The key distinguishing factor' [between levels of response] was the extent to which candidates were able to assess the impact of their chosen lines. Some simply repeated the word "powerful" from the question, without really thinking about why [they found] the lines so powerful.'

How to analyse a poem [seen or unseen]

A list of ingredients, not a recipe

Firstly, what not to do: sometimes pupils have been so programmed to spot poetic features such as alliteration that they start analysis of a poem with close reading of these micro aspects of technique. This is never a good idea. A far better strategy is to begin by trying to develop an overall understanding of what you think the poem is about. While, obviously, all these poems are about relationships of some sort or other, the nature of these relationships vary widely what they have say about this topic is also highly varied. Once you've established the central concerns, you can delve into the poem's interior, examining its inner workings in the light of these. And you should be flexible enough to adapt, refine or even reject your initial thoughts in the light of your investigation. The essential thing is to make sure that whether you're discussing imagery or stanza form, sonic effects or syntax, enjambment or vocabulary, you always explore the significance of the feature in terms of meanings and effect.

Someone once compared texts to cakes. When you're presented with a cake the first thing you notice is what it looks like. Probably the next thing you'll do is taste it and find out if you like the flavour. This aesthetic experience will come first. Only later might you investigate the ingredients and how it was made. Adopting a uniform reading strategy is like a recipe; it sets out what you must, do step by step, in a predetermined order. This can be helpful, especially when you start reading and analysing poems. Hence in our first volume in *The Art of Poetry* series we explored each poem under the same subheadings of narrator, characters, imagery, patterns of sound, form & structure and contexts, and all our essays followed essentially the same direction. Of course, this is a reasonable strategy for reading poetry and will stand you in good stead. However, this present volume takes a different, more flexible approach, because this book is designed for students aiming for levels 7 to 9, or A to A* in old currency, and to reach the highest levels your work needs to be a bit more conceptual, critical and individual. Writing frames are useful for beginners, like stabilisers when you learn to ride a bike. But, if you wish to write top level essays you need to develop your own frames.

Read our essays and you'll find that they all include the same principle ingredients – detailed, 'fine-grained' reading of crucial elements of poetry, imagery, form, rhyme and so forth - but each essay starts in a different way and each one has a slightly different focus or weight of attention on the various aspects that make up a poem. Once you feel you have mastered the apprentice strategy of reading all poems in the same way, we strongly recommend you put this generic essay recipe approach to one side and move on to a new way of reading, an approach that can change depending on the nature of the poem you're reading.

Follow your nose

Having established what you think a poem is about - its theme and what is interesting about the poet's treatment of the theme [the conceptual bit] - rather than then working through a pre-set agenda, decide what you honestly think are the most interesting aspects of the poem and start analysing these closely. This way your response will be original [a key marker of a top band essay] and you'll be writing about material you find most interesting. In other words, you're foregrounding yourself as an individual, critical reader. These most interesting aspects might be ideas or technique based, or both.

Follow your own, informed instincts, trust in your own critical intelligence as a reader. If you're writing about material that genuinely interests you, your writing is likely to be interesting for the examiner too. And, obviously, take advice to from your teacher too, use their expertise.

Because of the focus on sonic effects and imagery other aspects of poems are often overlooked by students. It is a rare student, for instance, who notices how punctuation works in a poem and who can write about it convincingly. Few students write about the contribution of the unshowy function words, such as pronouns, prepositions or conjunctions, yet these words are crucial to any text. Of course, it would be a highly risky strategy to focus your whole essay on a seemingly innocuous and incidental detail of a poem. But coming at things from an unusual angle is as important to writing great essays as it is to the production of great poetry.

So, in summary, when reading a poem for the first time, such as when doing an 'unseen' style question, have a check list in mind, but don't feel you must follow someone else's generic essay recipe. Don't feel that you must always start with a consideration of imagery if the poem you're analysing has, for instance, an eye-catching form. Consider the significance of major features, such as imagery, vocabulary, sonic patterns and form. Try to write about these aspects in terms of their contribution to themes and effects. But also follow your nose, find your own direction, seek out aspects that genuinely engage you and write about these.

The essays in this volume provide examples and we hope they will encourage you to go your own way, at least to some extent, and to make discoveries for yourself. No single essay could possibly cover everything that could be said about any one of these poems; aiming to create comprehensive essays like this would be utterly foolish. And we have not tried to do so. Nor are our essays meant to be models for exam essays – they're far too long for that. They do, however, illustrate the sort of conceptualised, critical and 'fine-grained' exploration demanded for top grades at GCSE and beyond. There's always more to be discovered, more to say, space in other words for you to develop some original reading of your own, space for you to write your own individual essay recipe.

Writing Literature essays

The Big picture and the small

An essay itself can be a form of art. And writing a great essay takes time, skill and practice. And also expert advice. Study the two figures in the picture carefully and describe what you can see. Channel your inner Sherlock Holmes to add any deductions you are able to form about the image. Before reading what we have to say, write your description out as a prose paragraph. Probably you'll have written something along the following lines:

First off, the overall impression: this picture is very blurry. Probably this indicates that either this is a very poor-quality reproduction, or that it is a copy of a very small detail from a much bigger image that has been magnified several times. The image shows a stocky man and a medium-sized dog, both orientated towards something to their left, which suggests there is some point of interest in that direction. From the man's rustic dress (smock, breeches, clog-like boots) the picture is either an old one or a modern one depicting the past. The man appears to be carrying a stick and there's maybe a bag on his back. From all of these details we can probably deduce that he's a peasant, maybe a farmer or a shepherd.

Now do the same thing for picture two. We have even less detail here and again the  picture's blurry. Particularly without the benefit of colour it's hard to determine what we're seeing other than a horizon and maybe the sky. We might just be able to make out that in the centre of the picture is the shape of the sun. From the reflection, we can deduce that the image is of the sun either setting or rising over water. If it is dawn this usually symbolises hope, birth and new beginnings; if the sun is setting it conventionally symbolises the opposite – the end of things, the coming of night/ darkness, death.

If you're a sophisticated reader, you might well start to think about links between the two images. Are they, perhaps, both details from the same single larger image, for instance.

Well, this image might be even harder to work out. Now we don't even have a whole  figure, just a leg, maybe, sticking up in the air. Whatever is happening here, it looks painful and we can't even see the top half of the body. From the upside orientation, we might guess that the figure is or has fallen. If we put this image with the one above, we might think the figure has fallen into water as there are horizontal marks on the image that could be splashes. From the quality of this image we can deduce that this is an even smaller detail blown-up.

You may be wondering by now why we've suddenly moved into rudimentary art appreciation. On the other hand, you may already have worked out the point of this exercise. Either way, bear with us, because this is the last picture for you to describe and analyse. So, what have we  here? Looks like another peasant, again from the past, perhaps medieval (?) from the smock-like dress, clog-like shoes and the britches. This character is also probably male and seems to be pushing some wooden apparatus from left to right. From the ridges at the bottom left of the image we can surmise that he's working the land, probably driving a plough. Noticeably the figure has his back to us; we see his turned away from us, suggesting his whole concentration is on the task at hand. In the background appear to be sheep, which would fit with our impression that this is an image of farming. It seems likely that this image and the first one come from the same painting. They have a similar style and subject and it is possible that these sheep belong to our first character. This image is far less blurry than the other one. Either it is a better-quality reproduction, or this is a larger, more significant detail extracted from the original source. If this is a significant detail, it's interesting that we cannot see the character's face. From this we can deduce that he's not important in and of himself; rather he's a representative figure and the important thing is what he is and what he isn't looking at.

Okay, we hope we haven't stretched your patience too far. What's the point of all this? Well, let's imagine we prefixed the paragraphs above with an introduction, along the following lines: 'The painter makes this picture interesting and powerful by using several key techniques and details' and that we added a conclusion, along the lines of 'So now I have shown how the painter has made this picture interesting and powerful through the use of a number of key techniques and details'. Finally, substitute painter and picture for writer and text. If we put together our paragraphs into an essay what would be its strengths and weaknesses? What might be a better way of writing our essay?

Consider the strengths first off. The best bits of our essay, we humbly suggest, are the bits where we begin to explain what we are seeing, when we do the Holmes-like

deductive thinking. Another strength might be that we have started to make links between the various images, or parts of a larger image, to see how they work together to provide us more information. A corresponding weakness is that each of our paragraphs seems like a separate chunk of writing. The weaker parts of the paragraphs are where we simply describe what we can

see. More importantly though, if we used our comments on image one as our first paragraph we seem to have started in a rather random way. Why should we have begun our essay with that image? What was the logic behind that? And most importantly of all, if this image is an analogue for a specific aspect of a text, such as a poem's imagery or a novel's dialogue we have dived straight into to analysing this technical aspect before we're established any overall sense of the painting/ text. And this is a very common fault with GCSE English Literature essays. As we've said before and will keep saying, pupils start writing detailed micro-analysis of a detail such as alliteration before they have established the big picture of what the text is about and what the answer to the question they've been set might be. Without this big picture it's very difficult to write about the significance of the micro details. And the major marks for English essays are reserved for explanations of the significance and effects generated by a writer's craft.

Now we'll try a different and much better approach. Let's start off with the big picture, the whole image. The painting below is called *Landscape with the fall of Icarus*. It's usually attributed to the Renaissance artist, Pieter Breughel and was probably painted in the 1560s. Icarus is a character from Greek mythology. He was the son of the brilliant inventor, Daedalus. Trapped on Crete by the evil King Minos, Daedalus and Icarus managed to escape when the inventor created pairs of giant feathered wings. Before they took to sky Daedalus warned his son not to get too excited and fly too near the sun as the wings were held together by wax that might melt. Icarus didn't listen, however. The eventual result was that he plummeted back to earth, into the sea more precisely and was killed.

Applying this contextual knowledge to the painting we can see that the image is about how marginal Icarus' tragedy is in the big picture. Conventionally we'd expect any image depicting such a famous myth to make Icarus's fall the dramatic centre of attention. The main objects of this painting, however, are emphatically not the falling boy hitting the water. Instead our eye is drawn to the peasant in the centre of the painting, pushing his plough [even more so in colour as his shirt is the only red object in an otherwise greeny-yellow landscape] and the stately galleon sailing calmly past those protruding legs. Seeing the whole image, we can appreciate the significance of the shepherd and the ploughman looking up and down and to the left. The point being made is how they don't even notice the tragedy because they have work to do and need to get on with their lives. The animals too seem unconcerned. As W. H. Auden puts it, in lines from *Musée des Beaux Arts*, 'everything turns away / Quite leisurely from the disaster'.

To sum up, when writing an essay on any literary text do not begin with close-up analysis of micro-details. Begin instead with establishing the whole picture: What the text is about, what key techniques the writer uses, when it was written, what sort of text it is, what effects it has on the reader. Then, when you zoom in to examine smaller details, such as imagery, individual words, metre or sonic techniques you can discuss these in relation to their significance in terms of this bigger picture.

What would our art appreciation essay look like now?

Paragraph #1: Introduction – myth of Icarus, date of painting, the way our eyes is drawn away from his tragic death to much more ordinary life going around him. Significance of this – even tragic suffering goes on around us without us even noticing, we're too busy getting on with our lives.

Paragraph #2: We could, of course, start with our first figure and follow the same order as we've presented the images here. But wouldn't it make more logical sense to discuss first the biggest, more prominent images in the painting first? So, our first paragraph is about the ploughman and his horse. How his figure placed centrally and is bent downwards towards the ground and turned left away from us etc.

Paragraph #3: The next most prominent image is the ship. Also moving from right to left, as if the main point of interest in the painting is off in that direction. Here we could consider the other human agricultural figure, the shepherd and his dog and, of course, the equally oblivious sheep.

Paragraph #4: Having moved on to examining background details in the painting we could discuss the symbolism of the sun on the horizon. While this could be the sun rising, the context of the story suggests it is more likely to be setting. The pun of the sun/son going down makes sense.

Paragraph #5: Finally, we can turn our attention to the major historical and literary figure in this painting, Icarus and how he is presented. This is the key image in terms of understanding the painting's purpose and effect.

Paragraph #6: Conclusion. What is surprising about this picture. How do the choices the painter makes affect us as viewer/ reader? Does this painting make Icarus's story seem more pathetic, more tragic or something else?

Now, all you have to do is switch from a painting to a poem.

Big pictures, big cakes, recipes and lists of instructions; following your own nose and going your own way. Whatever metaphors we use, your task is to bring something personal and individual to your critical reading of poems and to your essay writing.

Writing about language

Poems are paintings as well as windows; we look at them as well as through them. As you know, special attention should be paid to language in poetry because of all the literary art forms poetry, in particular, employs language in a precise, self-conscious and distinctive way. Ideally in poetry, every word should count. Analysis of language falls into distinct categories:

- By diction we mean the vocabulary used in a poem. A poem might be composed from the ordinary language of everyday speech or it might use elaborate, technical or elevated phrasing. Or both. At one time, some words and types of words were considered inappropriate for the rarefied field of poetry. The great Irish poet, W. B. Yeats never referred to modern technology in his poetry, there are no cars, or tractors or telephones, because he did not consider such things fitting for poetry. When much later, Philip Larkin used swear words in his otherwise well-mannered verse the effect was deeply shocking. Modern poets have pretty much dispensed with the idea of there being an elevated literary language appropriate for poetry. Hence in the CIE anthology you'll find all sorts of modern, everyday language.

- Grammatically a poem may use complex or simple sentences [the key to which is the conjunctions]; it might employ a wash of adjectives and adverbs, or it may rely extensively on the bare force of nouns and verbs. Picking out and exploring words from specific grammatical classes has the merit of being both incisive and usually illuminating.

- Poets might mix together different types, conventions and registers of language, moving, for example, between formal and informal, spoken and written, modern and archaic, and so forth. Arranging the diction in the poem in terms of lexico-semantic fields, by register or by etymology, helps reveal underlying patterns of meaning.

- For almost all poems imagery is a crucial aspect of language. Broadly imagery is a synonym for description and can be broken down into two types, sensory and figurative. Sensory imagery means the words and phrases that appeal to our senses, to touch and taste, hearing, smell and sight. Sensory imagery is evocative; it helps to take us into the world of the poem to share the experience being described. Figurative imagery, in particular, is always significant. As we have mentioned, not all poems rely on metaphors and similes; these devices are only part of a poet's box of tricks, but figurative language is always important when it occurs because it compresses multiple meanings into itself. To use a technical term figurative images are polysemic - they contain many meanings. Try writing out the all the meanings contained in a metaphor in a more concise and economical way. Even simple, everyday metaphors compress meaning. If we want to say our teacher is fierce and powerful and that we fear his or her wrath, we can more concisely say our teacher is a dragon.

Writing about patterns of sound

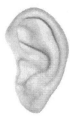

Like painters, some poets have powerful visual imaginations, while other poets have stronger auditory imaginations are more like musicians. And some poems are like paintings, others are more like pieces of music.

Firstly, what not to do: Tempting as it may be to spot sonic features of a poem and list these, don't do this. Avoid something along the lines of 'The poet uses alliteration here and the rhyme scheme is ABABCDCDEFEFGG'. Sometimes, indeed, it may be tempting to set out the poem's whole rhyme scheme like this. Resist the temptation: This sort of identification of features is worth zero marks. Marks in exams are reserved for attempts to link techniques to meanings and to effects.

Probably many of us have been sitting in English lessons listening somewhat sceptically as our English teacher explains the surprisingly specific significance of a seemingly random piece of alliteration in a poem. Something along the lines 'The double d sounds here reinforce a sense of invincible strength' or 'the harsh repetition of the 't' sounds suggests anger'. Through all our minds at some point may have passed the idea that, in these instances, English teachers appear to be using some sort of Enigma-style secret symbolic decoding machine that reveals how particular patterns of sounds have such definite encoded meanings.

And this sort of thing is not all nonsense. Originally deriving from an oral tradition, poems are, of course, written for the ear as much as for the eye, to be heard as much as read. A poem is a soundscape as much as it is a set of meanings. Sounds are, however, difficult to tie to very definite meanings and effects. By way of example, the old BBC Radiophonic workshop, which produced ambient sounds for radio and television programmes, used the same sounds in different contexts, knowing that the audience would perceive them in the appropriate way because of that context. Hence the sound of bacon sizzling of an audience clapping and of feet walking over gravel were actually recordings of an identical sound. Listeners heard them differently because of the context. So, we may, indeed, be able to spot the repeated 's' sounds in a poem, but whether this creates a hissing sound, yes like a snake, or the susurration of the sea will depend on the context within the poem and the ears of the reader. Whether a sound is soft and soothing or harsh and grating is also open to interpretation.

The idea of connecting these sounds to meanings or significance is a productive one. And your analysis will be most convincing if you use several pieces of evidence together. In other words, rather than try to pick out individual examples of sonic effects we recommend you explore the weave or pattern of sounds, the effects these generate and their contribution to feelings and ideas. For example, this might mean examining how alliteration and assonance are used together to achieve a particular mimetic effect.

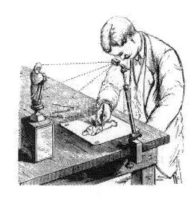

Writing about form & structure

As you know, there are no marks for simply identifying textual features. This holds true for language, sounds and also for form. Consider instead the relationship between a poem's form and its content, themes and effects. Form is not merely decorative or ornamental: A poem's meanings and effects are generated through the interplay of form and content. Broadly speaking the form can either work with or against a poem's content. Conventionally a sonnet, for instance, is about love, whereas a limerick is a comic form. A serious love poem in the form of a limerick would be unusual, as would a sonnet about an old man with a beard.

Sometimes poetic form can create an ironic backdrop to highlight an aspect of content. An example would be a formally elegant poem about something monstrous,  or a fragile form containing something robust or vice versa. Owen's sonnet, *Anthem for Doomed Youth* might spring to mind as the form of the sonnet sits uneasily with the idea of an anthem and also seems ironic for a poem about war. The artist Grayson Perry uses form in this ironic way. Rather than depicting the sort of picturesque, idealised images we expect of ceramics, Perry's pots and urns depict modern life in bright, garish colours. The urn pictured, for instance, is entitled *Modern Family* and depicts two gay men with a boy who they have presumably adopted. A thrash metal concert inside a church, a philosophical essay via text message, a fine crystal goblet filled with cherryade would be further examples of ironic relationships between message and medium, content and context or form.

****

Reading form

Put a poem before your eyes. Start off taking a panoramic perspective: Think of the forest, not the trees. Perhaps mist over your eyes a bit. Don't even read the words, just look at the poem, like at a painting. Is the poem slight, thin, fat, long, short?

What is the relation of whiteness to blackness? Why might the poet have chosen this shape? Does it look regular or irregular? A poem about a long winding river will probably look rather different from one about a small pebble, or should do. Unless form is being employed ironically. Now read the poem a couple of times. First time, fast as you can, second time more slowly and carefully. How does the visual layout of the poem relate to what it seems to be about? Does this form support, or create a tension against, the content? Is the form one you recognise, like a sonnet, or is it more open, more irregular like free verse? Usually the latter is obvious from the irregularity of the stanzas, line lengths and lack of metre or rhyme.

As Hurley and O'Neill explain in *Poetic Form: An Introduction*, like genre, form sets expectations: 'In choosing form, poets bring into play associations and expectations which they may then satisfy, modify or subvert'.[1] We've already suggested that if we see a poem is a sonnet or a limerick this recognition will set up expectations about the nature of the poem's content. The same thing works on a smaller level; once we have noticed that a poem's first stanza is a quatrain, we expect it to continue in this neat, orderly fashion. If the quatrain's rhyme scheme is xaxa, xbxb, in which only the second and fourth lines rhyme, we reasonably expect that the next stanza will be xcxc. So, if it isn't we need to consider why.

After taking in the big picture in terms of choice of form in relation to content zoom in: Explore the stanza form, lineation, punctuation, the use of enjambment and caesura. Single line stanzas draw attention to themselves. If they are end-stopped they can suggest isolation, separation. Couplets imply twoness. Stanzas of three lines are called tercets and feature in villanelles and terza rima. On the page, both these forms tend to look rather delicate, especially if separated from each other by the silence of white space. Often balanced through rhyme, quatrains look a bit more robust and sturdier. Cinquains are swollen quatrains in which the last line often seems to throw the stanza out of balance.

Focus in on specific examples and on points of transition. For instance, if a poem has four regular quatrains followed by a couplet, examine the effect of this change. If

---

[1] Hurley & O'Neill, *Poetic Form, An Introduction*, p.3

we've been ticking along nicely in iambic metre and suddenly trip on a trochee, examine why. Consider regularity. Closed forms of poems, such as sonnets, are highly regular with set rhyme schemes, metre and number of lines. The opposite form is called 'open', the most extreme version of which is free verse. In free verse poems, the poet dispenses with any set metre, rhyme scheme or recognisable traditional form. What stops this sort of poetry from being prose chopped up to look like verse? The care of the design on the page. Hence, we need to focus here on lineation. Enjambment runs over lines and makes connections; caesura pauses a line and separates words. Lots of enjambment generates a sense of the language running away from the speaker. Lots of caesuras generate a halting, hesitant, choppy movement to lines. Opposites, these devices work in tandem and where they fall is always significant in a good poem.

Remember poetic form is never merely decorative. And bear in mind too the fact that the most volatile materials require the strongest containers.

Nice to metre...

A brief guide to metre and rhythm in poetry

Why express yourself in poetry? Why read words dressed up and expressed as a poem? What can you get from poetry that you can't from prose? There are many compelling answers to these questions. Here, though, we're going to concentrate on one aspect of the unique appeal of poetry – the structure of sound in poetry. Whatever our stage of education, we are all already sophisticated at detecting and using structured sound. Try reading the following sentences without any variation whatsoever in how each sound is emphasised, and they will quickly lose what  essential human characteristics they have. The sentences will sound robotic. So, in a sense, we won't be teaching anything new here. It's just that in poetry the structure of sound is carefully unusually crafted and created. It becomes a key part of what a poem is.

We will introduce a few new key technical terms along the way, but the ideas are straightforward. Individual sounds [syllables] are either stressed [emphasised, sounding louder and longer] or unstressed. As well as clustering into words and sentences for meaning, these sounds [syllables] cluster into rhythmic groups or feet, producing the poem's metre, which is the characteristic way its rhythm works.

In some poems, the rhythm is very regular and may even have a name, such as iambic pentameter. At the other extreme a poem may have no discernible regularity at all. As we have said, this is called free verse. It is vital to remember that the sound in a good poem is structured so that it combines effectively with the meanings.

For example, take a look at these two lines from Marvell's *To his Coy Mistress*:

'But at my back I alwaies hear

Times winged Chariot hurrying near:'

Forgetting the rhythms for a moment, Marvell is basically saying at this point 'Life is short, Time flies, and it's after us'. Now concentrate on the rhythm of his words.

- In the first line every other syllable is stressed: 'at', 'back', 'al', 'hear'.
- Each syllable before these is unstressed 'But', 'my', 'I', 'aies'.
- This is a regular beat or rhythm which we could write
  ti TUM / ti TUM / ti TUM / ti TUM , with the / separating the feet. ['Feet' is the technical term for metrical units of sound]
- This type of two beat metrical pattern is called iambic, and because there are four feet in the line, it is tetrameter. So this line is in 'iambic tetrameter'. [Tetra is Greek for four]
- Notice that 'my' and 'I' being unstressed diminishes the speaker, and we are already prepared for what is at his 'back', what he can 'hear' to be bigger than him, since these sounds are stressed.
- On the next line, the iambic rhythm is immediately broken off, since the next line hits us with two consecutive stressed syllables straight off: 'Times' 'wing'. Because a pattern had been established, when it suddenly changes the reader feels it, the words feel crammed together more urgently, the beats of the rhythm are closer, some little parcels of time have gone missing.

A physical rhythmic sensation is created of time slipping away, running out. This subtle sensation is enhanced by the stress-unstress-unstress pattern of words that follow, 'chariot hurrying' [TUM-ti-ti, TUM-ti-ti]. So the hurrying sounds underscore the meaning of the words.

14 ways of looking at a poem

Though conceived as pre-reading exercises, most of these tasks work just as well for revision.

1. Mash them (1) – mix together lines from two or more poems. The students' task is to untangle the poems from each other.

2. Mash them (2) – the second time round make the task significantly harder. Rather than just mixing whole lines, mash the poems together more thoroughly, words, phrases, images and all, so that unmashing seems impossible. At first sight.

3. Dock the last stanza or few lines from a poem. The students should come up with their own endings for the poem. Compare with the poet's version. Or present the poem without its title. Can the students come up with a suitable one?

4. Break a poem into segments. Split the class into groups. Each group work in isolation on their segment and feedback on what they discover. Then their task is to fit the poem and their ideas about it together as a whole.

5. Give the class the first and last stanza of a poem. Their task is to provide the filling. They can choose to attempt the task at beginner level (in prose) or at world class level (in poetry).

6. Add superfluous words to a poem. Start off with obvious interventions, such as the interjection of blatantly alien, noticeable words. Try smuggling 'pineapple', 'bourbon' and 'haberdashers' into any of the poems and see if you can get it past the critical sensors.

7. Repeat the exercise – This time using much less extravagant words. Try to smuggle in a few intensifiers, such as 'really', 'very' and 'so'. Or extra adjectives.

8. Collapse the lineation in a poem and present it as continuous prose. The students' task is to put it back into verse. Discussing the various pros and cons or various possible arrangements – short lines, long lines, irregular lines - can be very productive. Pay particular attention to line breaks and the words that end them. After a whatever-time-you- deem-fit, give the class the pattern of the first stanza. They then have to decide how to arrange the next stanza. Drip feed the rest of the poem to them.

9. Find a way to present the shapes of each poem on the page without the words. The class should work through each poem, two minutes at a time, speculating on what the shape might tell us about the content of the poem. This exercise works especially well as a starter activity. We recommend you use two poems at a time, as the comparison helps students to recognise and appreciate different shapes.

10. Test the thesis that an astute reader can recognise poems by men from those written by women. Give the class one of the poems, such as *The Trees, The Trees are Down* or *Tears, Idle, Tears*, without the name of the poet. Ask them to identify whether the writer is male or female and to explain their reasons for identifying them as such. Obviously, for Tennyson's poem there's an interesting answer of a male writer writing in a female voice.

11. Split the class into groups. Each group should focus their analysis on a different feature of the poem. Start with the less obvious aspects: Group 1 should concentrate on enjambment and caesuras; group 2 on punctuation; group 3 on the metre and rhythm; group 4 on function words – conjunctions, articles, prepositions. 2-5 mins. only. Then swap focus, four times. Share findings.

12. In *Observations on Poetry*, Robert Graves wrote that 'rhymes properly used are the good servants whose presence at the dinner-table gives the guests a sense of opulent security; never awkward or over-clever, they hand the dishes silently and professionally. You can trust them not to interrupt the conversation or allow their personal disagreements to come to the notice of the guests; but some of them are getting very old for their work'. Explore the poets' use of rhyme in the light of Graves' comment. Are the rhymes ostentatiously original or old hat? Do they stick out of the poem or are they neatly tucked in? Are they dutiful servants of meaning or noisy disrupters of the peace?

13. The Romantic poet, John Keats, claimed that 'we hate poetry that has a palpable design upon us – and if we do not agree seems to put its hand its breeches pock'. Apply his comment to this selection of poems. Do any seem to have a 'palpable design' on the reader? If so, how does the poet want us to respond?

14. Each student should crunch the poem down to one word per line. Discuss this process as a class. Project the poem so the whole class can see it and start the crunching process by indicating and then crossing-out the function words from each line. Now discuss which of the remaining words is most important. This will also give you an opportunity to refer to grammatical terms, such as nouns and verbs. Once each line has been reduced to one word, from this list, pupils should crunch again. This time all that should remain are the five most important words in the whole poem. Now they need to write two or three sentences for each of these words explaining exactly why they are so important and why the poet didn't choose any of the possible synonyms.

'If I feel physically as if the top of my head were taken off, I know that is poetry'

EMILY DICKINSON

Emily Dickinson, *Because I Could Not Stop for Death*

There's a number of peculiar things about Dickinson's poetry and this rather Southern Gothic poem in particular. We might point to the fact that the poem appears to be narrated by an animated corpse, that death in the poem takes on the form of a civilised and gallant gentleman who takes the dead narrator out for a nice carriage ride in the country, as if on a first date. Then there's the fact that they are joined on their journey by a rather unusual guest or perhaps chaperone, 'Immortality'. However, putting those aside for a moment, the most

obvious examples of the oddities that initially puzzled Emily Dickinson's readers are her use of capital letters and dashes or hyphens [we'll call them dashes in the rest of this essay]. If you're a teacher, to help highlight these distinctive features, you could present the poem first to a class with them removed, only revealing Dickinson's eccentricities after the poem has been analysed. That way you can explore whether these features are mere curious adornments or whether they are more fundamental to the poem's meanings and effects.

'Because I could not stop for death
He kindly stopped for me.
The carriage held but just ourselves
And immortality.

We slowly drove, he knew no haste,
And I had put away
My labor and my leisure too,
For his civility.'

[and so forth]

Indeed, when the first publishers of Emily Dickinson's work came across her poems and their idiosyncrasies their instinct was to 'correct' them. The publishers did this by straightening the poems out and tidying them up, giving them titles, punctuating them more conventionally and even stretched their typically gaunt forms into more regular shapes. Only over time did readers come to realise that an essential part of this poet's artistic genius lay exactly in her unconventionality, and that idiosyncrasies such as her affection for dashes, were fundamental aspects of this originality. Not that there were, in fact, many publishers, or readers. During her lifetime [1830-1886] only about ten of Dickinson's poems were published. However, after the poet's death, her sister discovered a box containing numerous volumes full of poems. Over time, nearly two thousand poems, which had been carefully hand-stitched into little books, began to be published. And slowly Dickinson's reputation grew and grew. So much so that nowadays this famously reclusive poet is considered to be one of America's greatest poets and a feminist literary icon.

Telling it *slant*

Nearly everything in this poem is surprising. Take the first line: in what way and why could the narrator not 'stop' for death? Stop in what sense? The casual phrasing makes it seem that stopping for death, like stopping for a tea-break, is a matter of casual choice. Nevertheless, we might assume that the sense is that despite the narrator's efforts to avoid him, death has caught up with her. But the second line upsets this assumption. This is particularly due to the poet's use of the adverb 'kindly'. Either this implies that death has come as a relief and the narrator is

thankful, or that she is being bitterly ironic. From the rest of the poem, it seems the former is more likely and she means what she says. Next thing we know the narrator and death go for a leisurely ride in his carriage. Conventionally death is depicted as the grim reaper, of course. In Dickinson's poem the reaper seems to have left his scythe at home, thrown off his hooded gown and put on his best, most courteous

genteel manners. This death is not very grim. In fact, he's civil, like a Southern gentleman caller taking his belle out for a ride in the countryside. The narrator responds, as she should in all courtesy, by giving him all her attention, putting aside both her 'labor' and her 'leisure'. Peculiarly, at no point does the narrator express any fear or resistance to being taken for this ride by death.

Their journey takes them out of town and through time. They pass children and the school, pass the fields and journey on beyond the 'Setting Sun'. Children obviously indicate the start of life; the field is a place or work and where harvests are collected and the 'setting sun' suggests old age. The narrator reminds us of how ill-prepared for the journey she is in her light summer clothes of 'gossamer' and 'tulle', indicating that death caught up with her unexpectedly. At this point in the journey she still can feel physical sensations, so she has a corporeal body and is not yet a ghost or spirit. She shivers, but not, it seems, through fear.

Dickinson has defamiliarised death; now she defamiliarises the grave; it is a 'house' with architectural features, such as a 'roof' and a 'cornice' [perhaps the gravestone?] And then, in just four words time accelerates at warp drive and 'centuries' pass in a couple of metrical beats. Though the speaker has been long dead, it seems to her a short time, shorter than a 'day'. As Dickinson was brought up in a highly religious, strict puritan society, we'd expect death to lead to the resurrection and then on to heaven. Yet at the end of the poem the dead narrator has not been resurrected, even though she has been long dead. Instead she is aware of 'eternity' and even now she may not have reached this state, as the 'Horses' Heads' of the carriage are journeying '*toward* Eternity' but perhaps haven't got there yet. The unresolved ending of the poem indicates Dickinson's radical doubts about the truth of the Christian story of death and eternal resurrection.

The woman in white

Of course, there is a paradox here: The narrator appears to be dead and yet is still conscious of that fact and still thinking and speaking. One possible explanation is that Dickinson experienced a kind of death in life: Literary scholars are not certain about the exact facts, but the consensus is that when she was in her twenties the poet fell in love, probably with an older, married preacher called Charles Wadsworth.

Though she shared some precious time with Wadsworth, it seems her love was not, alas, requited. Soon after Wadsworth moved far away Dickinson became a recluse, hardly seeing any visitors and dressing always in a white. In her letters from around this time the poet also wrote that she 'had a terror' that may have precipitated some sort of breakdown. The relation between unrequited love and the 'terror' isn't clear. Other scholars argue that Dickinson consciously withdrew from the outside world because she  felt alienated by its attitudes and behaviour. Whether her withdrawal from the world was a rational decision, whether it was triggered by rejection in love or by some kind of existential terror, or any combination of these, we do not know. We do know she faced some sort of crisis and became a recluse. Clearly, however, in this poem the beau figure of Wadsworth, or some other gallant Southern gentleman, has been usurped by the figure of Death. In some ways it's as if the experience of love was like death for the poem's speaker - in some ways love seems to have killed her.

For a poem about the experience of death on the surface it seems remarkably calm and composed, almost, in fact, serene. Arranged into six orderly quatrains of fairly regular ballad or hymn metre [alternating lines of tetrameter and trimeter] the poem looks fairly conventional. But even before we add the dashes and capital letters we can see that Dickinson deviates from convention in the poem's rhyme scheme. In ballad metre the second and fourth lines of each quatrain should rhyme. Dickinson's scheme appears more erratic and random than a conventional pattern. After the first stanza she either uses no rhymes or slight rhymes, such as 'chill' and 'tulle', 'than the day' and 'eternity'. The expectation of sonic resolution, sonic closure, set up by the metre and stanza form is denied by Dickinson's errant rhyme scheme. But it is the capitalisation and the dashes most especially that really set Dickinson's poem apart from convention. So now it's time to show the class the poem with these features back in place.

Naturally the reader's eye is drawn to the capitalised words, like weeds among pavement slabs, as one critic has said. Picking them up gives the skeleton of the poem:

DEATH - CARRIAGE - OURSELVES - IMMORTALITY- HE - HIS - CIVILITY - SCHOOL - CHILDREN - RECESS - RING - FIELDS - GRAZING - GRAIN - SETTING - SUN - HE - US - DEWS - CHILL - GOSSAMER - GOWN - TIPPET - TULLE - HOUSE - SWELLING - GROUND - ROOF - CORNICE - CENTURIES - DAY - HORSES'S HEADS - ETERNITY

Mostly these words are concrete nouns, physical objects that exist in the world. They indicate the familiar world in which Dickinson lived - clothes, sky, weather, the town. There's a sprinkling too of abstract nouns too, big concepts, such as 'death', 'immortality' and 'eternity'. The list neatly summarises how Dickinson creates an unsettling atmosphere in her poem by combining the concrete and familiar with words that are mysterious, abstract and hard to conceptualise. <u>What though of the dashes? What do they contribute to the poem?</u>

Obviously, the grammatical function of a dash or a hyphen is to link words or phrases together. In Dickinson's hand-written manuscripts she uses them in a wide

variety of ways, and places, and sometimes they even appear at angles, even vertically. In *Because I Could not Stop for Death* Dickinson uses dashes liberally, insistently and almost obsessively. Dashes appear in two distinct places, with apparently distinct functions. Internal dashes create pauses for the reader, slowing and breaking up the movement of the verse, as if conveying hesitance, or even resistance to the direction the narrative inevitably must take. In this way they could be read as providing a counterbalance to the apparently serene acceptance of death by the poem's narrator, bumps or pauses on the smoothe journey out of town and to the grave. Dashes at the ends of lines create a chain of loose links between lines and over stanzas. But visually the right-hand side of each dash connects only to the white space at the side of the page, as if trying to link to something either not there or invisible. The effect is especially striking in the final line of the poem which finishes with a dash after 'Eternity', connecting that word and the entire poem to endless nothingness and silence. Again, rather than closure, there is an open-endedness. Perhaps this final blank, unresolved nothingness was the source of Dickinson's terror.

In summary, the poem presents death in a highly unusual way. The now dead narrator seemed to almost welcome death who appeared as a Southern gentleman caller and she offered no resistance to being taken away. Where the narrator ends up is unclear. They may be in eternity, or still heading towards it. And what happened to their chaperone, Immortality? Somewhere along the journey he/she/it seems to have exited the carriage, quietly and seemingly unnoticed.

['Crunching' a poem entails reducing it to the single most important word per line. Which word is the most important is obviously a matter of potential critical debate]

Because I Could not Stop for Death crunched:

DEATH - KINDLY - CARRIAGE - IMMORTALITY - SLOWLY - I - LABOR - CIVILITY - CHILDREN - RECESS - FIELDS - SETTING - US - CHILL - GOWN - TULLE - SEEMED - SWELLING - ROOF - GROUND - CENTURIES - SHORTER - SURMISED - ETERNITY

Elizabeth Bishop, *One Art*

Describe the poetic form of a villanelle in words and it sounds fiendishly difficult to write. Here are the authors of *The Making of a Poem, a Norton Anthology of Poetic Forms* giving it their best shot:

'Five stanzas occur of three lines each. They are followed by a stanza, a quatrain, of four lines. This is common to all villanelles. The first line of the first stanza serves as the last line of the second and fourth stanzas. The third line of the first stanza serves as the last line of the third and fifth stanzas. And these two refrain lines reappear to constitute the last two lines of the closing quatrain...The rhyme scheme is aba, for the first three lines of the poem. And these rhymes reappear to match and catch the refrains, throughout the villanelle. The first line of the first stanza rhymes with the third line of the fourth stanza. And so on.'[2]

Got it? Good. So your task now is to write your own villanelle. Except that the

 complex form of the villanelle seems to have bewitched even the august authors of the Norton guide. Because that's not quite right. The rhyme scheme in a villanelle is, indeed, aba, but this scheme runs through all the five three line, tercet, stanzas before finally being recycled in the concluding two lines. In other words, all the

rhymes in a villanelle are composed from just two rhyme sounds. Lines, 1, 3, 4, 6, 7,

---

[2] Strand & Boland, *The Making of a Poem*, p. 7

9, 10, 12, 13, 15, 16, 18 & 19 all rhyme with each other. The middle lines of each tercet, lines 2, 5, 8, 11, 14 and 17, also all rhyme with each other. Clearer now? Good. So your task is to write your own villanelle. Except that, we think it's much easier to appreciate the form of a villanelle through a visual representation, thus:

Line 1	A	1st refrain
Line 2	B	
Line 3	A	2nd refrain
Line 4	A	
Line 5	B	
Line 6	A	1st refrain (same as line 1)
Line 7	A	
Line 8	B	
Line 9	A	2nd refrain (same as line 3)
Line 10	A	
Line 11	B	
Line 12	A	1st refrain (same as lines 1 & 6)
Line 13	A	
Line 14	B	
Line 15	A	2nd refrain (same as lines 3 & 9)
Line 16	A	
Line 17	B	
Line 18	A	1st refrain (same as lines 1,6 & 12)
Line 19	A	2nd refrain (same as lines 3, 9 & 15)

The Art of the villanelle is hard to master

Now you've seen the form, time for you... except that it helps to try to think of a suitable subject that might fit this elegant, looping dance of a form with its repeated patterns of lines. What we need is a subject in which there is a lot of repetition, but with variations. How about a school day? And though the form looks devilishly difficult, actually, as the opening lines are recycled through the rest of the poem, once you've got your first three lines you've already written nearly half your poem, including the last two lines! It's helpful to write these lines in their positions once you've got your first three in place. By way of encouragement we've had a go at writing a villanelle, albeit loosely based on Bishop's, and you can find it at the back of this book.

Of course, Bishop's poem is a superlative example of a villanelle. Look, for example, at the inventiveness of her rhyming. Particularly impressive are rhymes like 'my last or' and 'was you meant' where the poet has had to use several words to match the sound of the matching single rhyme word. As there are only two of rhyme sounds, in a villanelle the whole sense of the poem can easily become warped by the strictness of the rhyme scheme and/or rhymes can stick out like a sore thumb, and the whole poem can sound contrived. If you try to write one, you'll likely appreciate what we mean. Dexterously Bishop uses enjambment and caesuras to flex the shape a little. Sentences run over the ends of lines and stop and start in the middle of others. A good example is the second and third lines of the third stanza where the rhyme is bedded down within a sentence, so the sound is muted as we almost run over it:

'places, and names, and where it was you meant
to travel. None of these...'

More than these technical skills, however, it is Bishop's use of the key repeating lines that really sets her poem apart from less brilliant villanelles. As we read through the poem these same, recycled lines take on different meanings, modulated by the context around them. So much so, that by the end they almost mean the opposite of what they first appeared to say.

Giving nothing away

As con men, magicians and every good literature student doth know, appearances can be deceptive. Look at Bishop's poem on the page and it seems neatly arranged, calm, regular, composed. And, indeed, it takes a lot of composure to write a villanelle. It's an exacting form that makes harder demands of the brain than the heart - the mathematical, pattern making muscles of the poetic imagination are given a good workout by a villanelle. With a villanelle it is always the form that comes first; the emotions and the words and the rhymes have to fit within its strict dance of recycled lines. The poem's declarative first line appears to confirm the poem's appearance of control and good order. Firstly, it's neatly arranged into regular iambic pentameter [stressed syllables are in bold]:

'The **art** of **los**ing **isn**'t **hard** to **mas**ter'.

A brisk rhythm and brusque tone are generated by an emphatic stress pattern ['the, of, -ing, -n't and '-er are obviously unstressed syllables]. The effect is underscored by assonantal rhyme of 'art', 'hard' and 'master' [though, we concede, a Northern accent would shorten the last vowel]. And the meaning is reassuring too. The line tells us plainly and directly that the intellect can triumph over emotions, that loss can be mastered, a mastery the villanelle itself seems to enact. The tone sounds assured, even, perhaps, a little flippant about this control the brain wields over the heart.

Our impressions appear to be confirmed by the rest of the first tercet. The poet is referring to the loss of inconsequential, trivial 'things' and there is a comic element to the idea that these things deliberately lose themselves. For anyone who has do family washing, lost socks might come to mind. And then the poet assures us that these sorts of losses are minor irritations at worst, certainly not disasters. This impression is confirmed by the satisfying closure created by the full rhyme of 'master' with 'disaster', a close underlined by the emphatic full stop at the end of the stanza.

For contemporary American readers Bishop's breezy opening lines may have been more striking due to their stark difference from the confessional poetry which was then all the rage. Confessional poetry, as the name implies, expressed the private or darker aspects of the poet's life experiences - their guilts, and their hang-ups, their issues and their addictions, in a direct, seemingly unfiltered, no-holds-barred style. Though Bishop's poem is written in the first person, the pronoun 'I' is withheld for a while, and the self-assured, measured, almost nonchalant, voice seems detached from any trauma its speaker may have suffered.

As Bishop's poem progresses, it appears to become a kind of sensible instruction manual about how to cope with loss. Losing stuff is an inevitable part of experience, the poem seems to be saying, and this poem will tell us how to accommodate ourselves to these minor losses. Hence in the second stanza the poet uses imperatives: 'Lose something every day. Accept the fluster'. 'Fluster' might be mildly annoying, bothersome, but we're not talking about any real distress here and the things lost, as before, are relatively trivial, just 'lost-door keys', an 'hour badly spent'. Repetition of the refrain in the last line of this stanza emphasises the point that really it's not hard to master these sorts of inconsequential losses.

Harder to master

Perhaps by this point in our reading of the poem we get a sense of some kind of disturbance underneath the apparently serene surface of the words. Repeating the 'art of losing', for instance, might make us pause and reflect on the phrase a bit more. How exactly could 'losing' be like an art? Moreover, why would we need to 'master' this art if all we are doing is getting used to losing trivial things? Perhaps too the half-rhyme of 'fluster' and 'master' means the second stanza doesn't end with quite the same assured harmony as the first one did.

More questions are prompted by the third stanza. Why do we need to practice losing? What does losing 'farther' or 'faster' entail? Does the former mean a permanent, or perhaps more significant, loss? By 'faster' does the poet mean letting go of more things, more often? And there is another escalation. Now the ill-defined 'things' and 'something' have become more specific, 'places' and "names". How do you lose a place? Perhaps by being forcibly taken away from somewhere. Losing 'names' might mean losing track of details, as people sometimes do as they get older. Perhaps this poem is about aging, or even about developing some sort of mental illness that leads to a lot of forgetting, such as dementia, perhaps. But losing 'names' could also stand in for losing people from your life. With its strong, pentametric stride, the last line of the third stanza should sound reassuring: 'None of these will bring disaster'. But it doesn't entirely convince. By being repeated, that word 'disaster' demands more of our attention and becomes more ominous.

In the succeeding stanzas the list of losses pile up: Precious, intimate things, such as the speaker's mother's 'watch', their beloved 'houses' and quite suddenly the scale is huge, and they are losing 'cities', 'realms' a 'continent'. Almost the world, in fact. The measured, distant, even off-hand voice has been supplanted, almost entirely, by a much more personal one: 'I lost'. And this new voice tells us how the speaker felt about these things - 'loved houses', 'lovely' cities and it directs us to 'look!', as if taken by surprise, or horrified. By now, the reader is probably thinking that those two holding phrases, the recycled lines, are coming under a lot of strain. It's as if the poet protests too much, and the words start to sound hollow: 'But it wasn't a disaster'. By now it seems rather like these things must, in fact, be a series of disasters. Either the poet is putting on a brave face, or she is trying to convince herself, repeating the comforting pattern of words, like running beads of a rosary through her fingers. But they no longer really believe these words.

It wasn̶'̶t̶ a disaster

Judging from the opening few tercets of this villanelle it would be hard to believe that Bishop's poem was prompted by the breakup of a relationship and the failed suicide attempt that followed, involving alcohol and an overdose of sleeping pills. And if we'd assumed that this poet had lived an untroubled life from her nonchalant, breezy tone, or even that she had sailed serenely through some troubled biographical waters, we'd be much, much mistaken. Bishop was a poet who suffered many terrible losses. Her father died in her early infancy and her mother was separated from her daughter and committed to a mental hospital while the poet was still a small child [information that makes the reference to the lost watch far more poignant]. The young Bishop suffered from a variety of debilitating illness and she was passed between different members of the family, living in different places, not all of them nurturing homes. In fact, she was the victim of sexual abuse by one of her uncles.

Bishop was also a lesbian, but kept that fact a secret her whole life, despite being a writer! And despite high achievements, such as winning the coveted Pulitzer Prize, and holding an academic post at Harvard, she struggled with depression and alcoholism for much of her life. Rather than mastering loss, sometimes it seems she sought to obliterate it.

Nor would we guess that *One Art* went through seventeen drafts to arrive at the seemingly effortlessly accomplished final version. Clearly then it was, in fact, a terrible struggle to master the 'art of losing'. Perhaps wrestling the poem into control was a way for Bishop to wrestle all the losses her life had accumulated into some sort of holding pattern, even, perhaps to transmute them into art. Surely this is the mastery of the creative will over disaster.

Finally, in the final stanza this real trauma breaks through the poem's even surface. The tight rhyme scheme, that has kept the emotions in check, loosens. The punctuation becomes more erratic and pronounced; a hyphen after a full stop, succeeded by a capital letter, two sets of brackets, as if unruly thoughts have popped up unbidden. Check back and you'll notice the smoothe flow of the verse is broken up by caesuras in every tercet other than the first. Here too we stop after the significant verb 'lied'. Though the speaker says she 'shan't have lied' and uses factual, unemotional language, 'it's evident', this sentiment is belied by the emotional command - of the will to the poetic self - in the last line '(*Write* it!)'. The clenched teeth  determination is emphasised by the italics, capitalisation and the exclamation mark.

Why doesn't she want to write it? Placing this instruction at that exact point in the line isolates the last two words from the context of the line and the rest of a poem that has sought all the way through to diffuse and bury and manage their devastating emotional violence. The last line of the poem cannot hide the fact that the loss of this beloved has been 'like disaster'.

On the verge

So, this is a love poem. A poem about the loss of love and the poet's devastation. Why didn't Bishop express these emotions more directly? Why go about pretending that it is easy to cope with such loss when clearly it wasn't? Well, isn't it more powerful this way? We read the last line, and this throws a whole new light over the rest of the poem. Reading it again, we more easily detect the clues that the speaker's bravery was a sort of front, a way of trying to cope with devastation. Bishop's emotional restraint makes us read between the lines and work things out for ourselves, engaging us as readers. By the end we understand that accepting small loses was a way to try to inoculate herself. This, after all, is how we protect ourselves against deadly diseases.

And less sometimes can be more. A young playwright once said it took them a few plays to realise that it was always more dramatically effective to show someone on the verge of tears, rather than someone crying. This is because crying releases tension. On the verge of tears, when emotion is only just held in check, means there's two contrary forces at work, an internal conflict, a holding on as well as a letting go. A good actor is able to allow us to see glimpses of hidden pain beneath a broad smile, show us the effort of keeping up appearances.

There are two opposing forces at work in Bishop's poem. The catastrophic emotional heart of the thing, is the experience of multiple, obliterating losses. But this is countered and checked by the forces of the will and reason. But it's an even fight; it could go either way. And written this way, the poet shows us her courage, her grit, her resilience. She does not simply slip easily into despair. She tries hard to convince herself that she can immure herself to loss, inoculate herself with small doses, so that she copes with the really big losses in the past and now in the present. Isn't this far more admirable and powerful than a confessional style poem that just lets all the emotion rip? *One Art* dramatises a holding on as well as a letting go, articulates the deep trauma beneath an ordered surface, the agony beneath a serene smile.

One Art crunched:

LOSING - SEEM - DISASTER - FLUSTER - KEYS - MASTER - PRACTICE - NAMES - NONE - MOTHER'S - LOVED - LOSING - CITIES - CONTINENT - MISS - YOU - EVIDENT - HARD - DISASTER

Alfred, Lord Tennyson, *Song: Tears, Idle Tears*

Sweetly plangent flow[3]

Scan the first line of Tennyson's blank verse poem and you might notice something rather odd. This is how I'd scan it [stressed syllables are in bold]:

'Tears, **id**le **tears**, I **know** not **what** they **mean**'

See what I mean? The first time the key word 'tears' is mentioned it is sonically diminished, merely an unstressed syllable before '**id**le'. The second time it appears, however, 'tears' is sonically picked out, stressed by the metrical pattern. We have also been primed to notice it by the fact that it is repeated so soon. So the first time the word is made sonically insignificant, the second time the opposite happens. The uncertainty generated here by the metre is repeated in the poem's second line, which starts with the phrase 'Tears from the depth'. Now this could be scanned as either a trochee [stress, unstress] followed by two iambs [unstress, stress]: '**Tears** from the **depth**'. In which case it would have bucked the pattern laid down by the fully iambic first line. Alternatively, it could just as well be read as standard iambic, which, after all, is the pattern of the rest of the line:

'Tears **from** the **depth** of **some** di**vine** de**spair**'

---

[3] This phrase is from the influential critic F.R. Leavis's critique of the poem.

But, even if the line is scanned as being iambic, the simple fact that we have heard the word 'tears' repeated, now for the third time, makes us notice it and gives it significance. Perhaps you are thinking this all seems rather abstruse and incidental, the sort of classic over reading trap English teachers are prone to fall into. Perhaps you're puzzled by us starting with such micro-analysis before we have established the 'big picture'. But stick with it. Consider how easily Tennyson could have avoided these uncertain patterns. The first line, for instance, could have been regularised as: 'My **tears**, such **idle tears,** what **can** they **mean'**, or some such arrangement. Consider too that Tennyson was an absolute master craftsman, the greatest poet of the Victorian age, known for his dexterity with metre, syntax and diction. Then, you might at least concede, that the poet starts this poem off in a way that is deliberately uncertain and that this uncertainty is encoded into both the metre and syntax of its first two lines.

Uncertainty is not only expressed through the metre and syntax, of course. It's there too in the diction, most obviously in the oxymoronic 'divine despair'. How can despair, the absolute loss of any hope, ever be 'divine'? Something divine is heavenly, perfect, joyful. More subtly, there's also semantic tension between the adjective 'idle' and the run of alliterative words in the second line, 'depth' and 'divine despair'. There's a number of possible meanings of 'idle' in play - lazy, not working, inactive, pointless, without foundation - with the latter two here seeming best to fit the context. But the second line gives us the foundation, the source and cause of the tears. The tears cannot be lazy reactions or pointless if they are expressions of deep, mixed emotions.

No wonder that the poet says he does not 'know' what these tears 'mean'. He seems more than confused, more like he's being pulled in opposite directions, or stronger than that, riven by extremes. To say his feelings are ambivalent would be an understatement. For the cause of this deep, albeit divine, despair is, surprisingly not the death of a loved one, or some horrible trauma. No, it is seeing 'happy' fields! Now, fields cannot be 'happy' or 'unhappy', so the personifying adjective is a projection from the observer onto the observed. So, despair is prompted by happiness? That really does seem perverse and contradictory. Further mixed messages: the fields are 'autumn', not 'spring', the latter a season more commonly associated with happiness. But perhaps it is what lies behind this image of happy fields that really prompts the lovely agonising that animates Tennyson's verse, 'thinking of days that are no more'. Perhaps this is the key to the paradoxical quality of the rest of the first stanza and, indeed, the whole poem.

Remembering a happy time might rekindle that happiness. But if that time is in the irrecoverable past and things have changed since them, this happiness may be surrounded by sadness. That does help to explain the 'divine despair' oxymoron, but it doesn't really address why Tennyson labels his tears with the pejorative adjective 'idle'. An extract from a highly useful website from Cambridge Authors, however, helps illuminate this issue:

...Tennyson's age was one of 'purposeful didacticism, useful toil and useful knowledge'. Perhaps, Professor Glen suggests, 'Tears, idle tears' may be seen as 'a riposte' or 'counterpoint to that rhetoric of progress' which characterised Tennyson's era.[4]

In other words, in this poem Tennyson is thinking about the possible value of such 'idleness', such thinking about thinking, such apparent indulging in emotions, and whether it can in any way be productive or justified in terms of the Victorian virtue of usefulness. Certainly, with all due respect, whatever the great F.R. Leavis might have written, what we haven't got in this first stanza, or indeed, in the rest of the poem is a merely 'sweetly plangent flow'. Underneath the smooth flow of the surface of the verse are powerful rip tides, pulling the poem and its interpretation in different directions.

Riven by opposites

Other examples of these rip tides can be found throughout the poem. Take the second stanza. It opens with an image that suggests the power of imagination and of memory can almost transcend time. The speaker sees an image of dead friends recalled from the 'underworld' as if it is as 'fresh as the first beam glittering on a sail'. But this image of shiny newness is mirrored and countered in the following lines.

---

[4] http://www.english.cam.ac.uk/cambridgeauthors/tennyson-tears-idle-tears-4/

'Sad' replaces 'fresh'; 'last' replaces 'first'; instead of the 'glittering' brilliant light of a new day, the light 'reddens' as the day ends and images of rising 'up' are replaced by ones of sinking down. In the following stanza, 'dark' modulates 'dawns', a symbol more usually associated with the coming of light, and two images of life and light, one aural the other visual ['half-awakened birds' and the 'glimmering square' of the window] are countered by two matching images of death, 'dying ears' and 'dying eyes'.

What is real, what is imagined, what is remembered are radically confused in the final, ambiguous stanza. It may take us a while, for example, to decipher the first line  as it could mean that kisses are dearer to us once we are dead. Moreover, these kisses are as 'sweet' as those 'hopeless fancy feigned' [my italics]. So, these second kisses are not real, but projections, simulations of the imagination ['fancy'] and the first kisses are as 'sweet' as imaginary kisses. And they are 'on lips that are for others'. Who are these others? Does 'feigned' refer backwards to the kisses or forward to the lips, or to both? What is real, what is ghostly and what is imaginary here? The following adjectival phrase, 'deep as love' presumably refers back to the 'remembered kisses' but could equally refer forward. The two semi-colons offer little help navigating how the phrases relate to each other. 'Wild with all regret' doesn't seem to fit easily either. Though we may connect 'regret' with the loss of the beloved [and their kisses] the animated adjective 'wild' is at odds with others used in the rest of the stanza, 'dear', 'sweet' and 'hopeless'. Finally, of course, we arrive at a closing oxymoronic phrase 'O death in life' that conflates the two ultimate absolutes about existence. Rather than a 'sweetly plangent flow' it seems the verse is deliberately convoluted, almost tortured by the forces pulling it in contrary directions.

Loops of language

In addition to the contradictory language that we have just made such heavy weather of tracing in the poem, the other dominant characteristic is repetition. Repetition occurs at:

- word level, within and across lines, over stanzas
- in the semantics of the imagery
- in the form of the poem.

Individual words are repeated, sometimes very soon after each other. For example, 'tears', 'fresh', 'sad', 'strange', 'dying', 'deep' and 'love'. As we have seen, the images in the poem oscillate between describing newness, life and light and aging, darkness and death. Tennyson also employs a refrain at the end of each stanza. Acting as a summary of the previous four lines, each time this refrain ends with the same six words 'the days that are no more'. In addition, enhancing the pattern of returning and recycling, words from the rest of the stanza are repeated, and, in the middle two stanzas are repeated in the same syntactical pattern; 'So sad, so fresh', 'so sad, so strange' with only a slight modulation. And, of course, each stanza has five, unrhymed lines of pentameter, each ending with the same word and a full stop. It is rather like as we move forward through reading the poem we are caught in loops that arrest our progression and even take us backwards. Thus embodied in the form of the poem is the idea of subjective time. Vivid memory, for a moment of two, has the power to undo time, to bring back the past into the present. Whether this is a productive power or whether it entraps the writer and the speaker in 'idle' emotion, we'll have to leave you to decide.

Song, Tears, Idle Tears crushed:

TEARS - DESPAIR - HEART - HAPPY - NO - FRESH - FRIENDS - SAD - BELOW - MORE - STRANGE - EARLIEST - DYING - GLIMMERING - SAD - KISSES - FEIGNED - LOVE - WILD - DEATH

In all fairness to Mr. Leavis we can see how he arrived at his reading of the poem as a melancholy reverie. The dominant repeated adjective, after all, is 'sad'. The lack of rhyme also contributes to a downbeat, possibly plaintive mood. Clearly Tennyson is thinking about how we carry our memories and our past about with us and how these can impinge on the present and colour our emotions. But what he has to say about this is, I feel, more complex than a simple lament for what has past. If you like the poem and are interested enough, you might want to discover its context within the frame poem of *The Princess*, a context that will further enrich your appreciation of this one.

For instance, putting Tennyson's poem back into is original literary context reveals that the anonymous speaker or weeper of *Tears, Idle Tears* is actually female.

 Victorian culture strictly demarcated the male and female spheres [men dominated the wider the world, whereas the female sphere was the domestic] and valorised an active, vigorous manliness. Hence the poet could be read as exploring the value of a distinctly female perspective and understanding of experience. If you're a teacher, you could experiment with the voice of the poem by presenting it first to a class without the name of the poet. Ask them to guess whether the writer or speaker is female or male and to determine when the poem might have been written. Though the phrasing might be Victorian, the imagery and diction seems rather timeless.

Stephen Spender, *My Parents*

Alongside the pre-eminent W.H. Auden, Stephen Spender [1909-1995] was part of a group of socially and politically engaged poets who found fame in the 1930s. A one-time member of the Communist party, Spender, like Auden, was left-leaning and socially progressive. Though he was married and had two children, Spender's sexuality was complex and he had relationships with men as well as women. As he wrote to his friend Christopher Isherwood [the writer whose work was adapted into the musical *Cabaret*] 'I fine boys more attractive'. Three characters appear in this short, three-stanzared poem; Spender's parents, the poet himself and the 'rough' kids. Though the poem is titled *My Parents* it focuses more on the poet's interaction with the rough children, as if they were a more powerful influence on his sense of self and exerted a stronger hold on his imagination. The poet's sense of identity is defined, in fact, through contrast to these common boys.

His middle-class parents

All parents probably at some point tell their children not to associate with a particular child or group of children who might look like trouble. It's understandable and natural for parents to want to protect their children, particularly from those who may do them harm. Spender's class-conscious poem, however, suggests that creating separate 'worlds' is unhealthy and only perpetuates division, misunderstanding and hostility. In the end, such division also perpetuates inequality. Perhaps one of the reasons why the rough kids bark like 'dogs' at the poet's 'world' is because they have been excluded from it. Despite fearing the children, the poet also seems to recognise qualities in them that he does not possess or he has lost.

The rough kids

First off, these kids are described simply as 'rough' and 'coarse', suggesting physical toughness and a lack of civilised manners. Clearly they're working class children and are very poor; Spender tells us they 'wore torn clothes' and 'rags'. Playing on the rhyme 'sticks and stones', a simile is used to signal their verbal roughness, their insults and aggression - they 'threw words like stones' and cruelly copied the poet's lisp. On the positive side, these children seem free and unencumbered by any awkward self-consciousness; they are physically active in a wide range of locations - running in the 'streets', 'climbing 'cliffs', 'tripping' by 'country streams', springing out from 'behind bushes'. They may be poor, but they are not malnourished; they are physically powerful [at least, in comparison to Spender] with 'muscles like iron' and they're 'lithe', like athletes. They are also a 'they'; a group of kids playing together in contrast to the isolated and perhaps lonely 'I' of the poet who can only watch and witness their collective fun.

The Spender kid

Though they treat him with disdain, the poet has ambivalent feelings about the rough kids. He 'feared' them 'more than tigers' which suggests a lot of fear. Twice he compares them to animals; they spring out 'like dogs to bark' at him. He also seems to have been physically and verbally abused by them with their words like weapons, their 'jerking hands' and 'knees tight' on his arms. As a child, the poet tried to be forbearing and Christian, turning his cheek when they throw mud at him. And in the last line he tells us plainly that 'he longed to forgive them'. Why? Because he is attracted to their physical energy and free-wheeling mischief - he admires, even envies them. Look at the verbs performed by the poet in *My Parents*: he 'feared', 'looked', he pretended and he 'longed'. He is 'kept' like a delicate exhibit in a museum. Compare those with the verbs describing the rough kids - 'threw', 'ran', 'climbed', 'tripped', 'copied', 'sprang'. There is also a definite homoerotic element too to the description of the rough children, with flashes of 'thighs' through clothes, and of their powerful 'muscles like iron'.

Bridge building

Winningly, Spender doesn't try to present himself in any sympathetic or heroic way in this autobiographical poem. Frankly he's timid and wimpy. A bullied victim of rougher, tougher kids, he seems a hesitant, sensitive, poetic soul. Nor does he sugar soap his description of the working-class boys. He tries to be honest and transparent about his class prejudice. Neither does he provide an easy solution to the class animosity he emblematises. Despite his willingness and desire to build bridges between their world and his, the rough kids 'never smiled' and so, at the end of the poem, there is no rapprochement.

Another way in which Spender tries to build bridges is in the style of his poem. Writing after the avant-garde elitism of modernism, Spender takes poetry in the opposite direction, making it accessible to a wider readership. On the page *My Parents* looks traditional and conventional, with three neat quatrains, that most familiar of stanza forms. The poem also reads like prose; there's no metre and Spender also eschews end-rhyme. Listen to him read it in his distinctly upper-middle class accent: https://www.youtube.com/watch?v=vqRn5tsxXXQ and you will, however, pick up some internal rhyme that gives the language a lyrical lilt. In particular, Spender uses alliteration and assonance to create a tight weave of sound, a good example being, 'threw **wo**rds like st**o**nes and **wo**re **to**rn cl**o**thes'. In addition to those devices, 'w' and 's' sounds bind the words closely together. Interestingly, listening to the poem also highlights a misprint in the CIE anthology: 'tripped by country streams' should read 'stripped', a verb that further supports a homoerotic reading of the poem.

Overall the poem's diction is composed of ordinary words and there are no elaborate metaphors or knowing intellectual allusions, none of the fragmentation and collage effects associated with modernism. It's a poem that tries to build bridges from the rarefied literary world to the world of these children and the common reader.

Spender was a poet who hoped to help make a better, fairer, less class-based world. Gently and quietly, self-deprecatingly his poem dramatises some of the difficulties of making that hope a reality.

My Parents crunched:

ROUGH - STONES - THIGHS - STRIPPED - FEARED - TIGHT - COARSE - LISP - SPRANG - DOGS - PRETENDING - LONGED

Fleur Adcock, *For Heidi with the Blue Hair*

A sympathetic voice

Who is the speaker of this conversation poem addressed to Heidi? Clearly, they are a close family member as they are familiar with intimate details of the story, such as exactly what the headmistress said and how Heidi and her father responded. They also hover like an invisible presence in the domestic scene in the kitchen. Clearly the speaker isn't Heidi's mother as we learn of her death in the fifth stanza, but they do take a caring, maternal attitude to the girl. Clearly, they are a sympathetic observer of the situation, siding it seems with Heidi's act of rebellion against society's norms and the school's rules, perhaps giving her a little emotional leeway because she is still a child, has suffered a traumatic loss and is still working through her grief. We might conjecture that the poem is written from the point of view of a close female relative, a grandmother or perhaps aunty. They're close enough to know what happened, close enough to express their support, but not close enough to be an active participant in this narrative. They can, however, shape the way we as readers respond to it.

An intimate conversation

Fleur Adcock is a New Zealand poet who lives in England. Identity is a major theme in her poetry and especially how our identities are shaped by nationality, culture, religion, family and gender. As in this poem, Adcock's poems often express a feminist perspective on experience. In addition to the narrator, For *Heidi with Blue Hair* features several other characters - namely Heidi, her friend, the school headmistress, Heidi's father and, 'behind the arguments', Heidi's dead mother.

Heidi's act of rebellion isn't just against the school rules, she is also breaking expectations based on her gender. Specifically she rejects expectations that young women should make themselves look attractive to the opposite sex. By dying her hair a non-naturalistic colour, 'ultramarine', shaving off the sides, like a military crew-cut, and finishing the look with 'jet-black spikes', Heidi adopts a style that is punky and deliberately unfeminine. Shaving and spikes are aggressive features, spikes in particular recalling weaponry. And the colour symbolism of 'jet-black' is obvious. Read sympathetically, as the school might and perhaps should have done, the haircut is the outward expression of Heidi's hurt - the anger, confusion and grief she must be feeling about her mother's premature death. Black and blue, her hair is an externalisation of her inner emotional bruise. Does it take more courage for a young woman to go against society's expectations, particularly in regard to her appearance, than it does for a young man? Yes, probably it still does. Hence the narrator and we, as readers, may admire the courage and individualism Heidi shows in rejecting social norms and gender stereotypes.

Heidi's interaction with society and its official institutions, embodied here by the school, reprises one of literature's oldest and most common themes, the relationships between the individual and society. Big questions hover in the background of the poem: To what extent should the individual be granted liberty to make their own choices, even if these might be harmful to themselves or to others? To what extent should  society enforce conformity to it values, norms and expectations? The poem doesn't propose answers to these fundamental questions, but Adcock does make it apparent which side she is on in these debates.

It seems it was significant to the poet that Heidi's friend was 'black'. Perhaps this is because the poem may be set in New Zealand and the girl's blackness would make her a minority in a predominantly white society. This girl expresses 'solidarity' in a 'witty' way and, if we weren't already sure, these positive, affirming comments and the poem's last line, 'the battle was won', underline which side the narrator is on.

Solidarity

All the way through the poem there have been indicators of the narrator's sympathetic bias and evidence of how she tries to influence readers to take the same side in the argument. The poem is, for instance, written 'for' Heidi, expresses solidarity with her and is addressed to her. More subtly, the use of the second person pronoun, 'you' and 'your', places readers in Heidi's shoes, encouraging us to identify with her. The narrative is also structured to privilege Heidi's side of the story. It starts with her and we spend considerably more time in the kitchen scene than we do in the school. Newspapers can be accused of 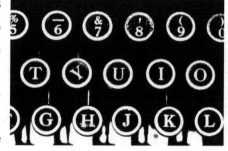 bias if they quote only for one side of a story. In Adcock's poem, the headmistress's version of events is conveyed only in reported speech - we never actually hear her voice. In contrast, we hear directly two voices from the other side. We are also told of the impact the school's decision to suspend Heidi has on her emotionally; she is in 'tears', which evokes our sympathy, and yet she also expresses defiance, 'not even if I wanted to', which we may again admire.

Predominantly the language in Adcock's poem is very ordinary and conversational, so much so, in fact, that she is able to incorporate actual direct speech quite naturally into the verse. Winningly, there's nothing inflated, obscure or showy about Adcock's style. Our attention is not being drawn egotistically to the poet's own brilliance through ostentatious imagery; instead the writer remains in the background and allows us to focus on the situation she outlines. The vocabulary is unfussy and straightforward and mostly it's also employed literally. Only twice does Adcock heighten the language into metaphor and both instances help to further tip the reader's sympathies towards Heidi.

Both instances occur in the crucial fifth stanza, the real heart of the poem and of the story. Specifically the death of Heidi's mother is described as having 'shimmered' 'behind the arguments'. The verb implies a ghostly, but inconstant projection of light. This imagery helps us to appreciate the continuing impact of the loss on Heidi's behaviour, and we surely must admire the sensitivity and decency of not using this trauma as an excuse to escape punishment from the school. In contrast, the last line of this stanza the teachers are said to have 'twittered' about the situation and then immediately afterwards given in. Comparing the teachers to small birds, the verb implies that their conversations were inconsequential. We certainly aren't going to hear what they might have said, because, really, it doesn't matter, the poet implies.

Behind the gentle and kindly sympathy of Adcock's narrator there's something a bit stronger and more steely. The poem sits squarely and solidly on the page; it's self-composed and doesn't feel it has to try too hard to please the reader. It expresses solidarity with the individual battling with their society, most especially when that individual is both young and female, and when society is rigidly insensitive and has deaf ear to grief. And Adcock's poem conveys hope that, despite the always uneven odds, these sorts of battles can, and will, be 'won'.

For Heidi crunched:

DYED - ULTRAMARINE - CLIPPED - SPIKES - SCHOOL - HEADMISTRESS - NOT - FORBIDDEN - ANYTHING - SCHOOL - TEARS - FREEDOM-LOVING - BEHAVIOUR - JUST - SCHOOL - ME - DAD - COST - WON'T - WATED - UNFAIR - DEATH - SHIMMERED - NOTHING - TWITTERED - FRIEND - WHITE - PRECISELY - SOLIDARITY - WON

Grace Nichols, *Praise Song for my Mother*

Firing up the imagination

Not all poems should be approached first through analytical methods, particularly if

you've quite a few to cover. The furniture game is a fun and creative way to help students to write half-decent poems. It works like this: each pupil should think of a famous person and keep their choice a secret. They then answer the following questions, writing them out in full sentences:

If I were a colour I'd be ....

If I were a vehicle I'd be a ....

If I were building I'd be a ....

If I were the weather I'd be a ....

If I were a sound I'd be a ....

If I were a flower I'd be a ....

If I were something in nature I'd be ....

If I was food I'd be ....

If I were a weapon I'd be ....

If I were an item of furniture I'd be ....

Obviously, you can add metaphors of your own invention. Once they've completed their answers, pupils can read out their poems and their classmates can try to guess the famous person from the description. Often weaker pupils choose associations rather than metaphors. So, for Lewis Hamilton that might say he is the colour black or that he's a formula one racing car. If this happens, it provides a good opportunity to reinforce their understanding of how metaphor involves an implicit comparison of two things. The last part of the challenge is to re-shape this draft into something more like a proper poem. To do this they could try to introduce a rhyme scheme with rhymes in every other line. They might need to rearrange syntax too, e.g. 'I'd be a Yorkshire pudding, if I were food'. Combining images in improbable ways also generates more interesting lines: 'I'm a Yorkshire pudding in a pin stripe suit' and so forth.

Go to your wide futures

As its title indicates, Grace Nichols'

unpretentious and tender poem celebrates a daughter's love for her mother. A separation has grown between the two characters in the poem and there are a few possible explanations for this: Maybe the separation arises from the poet growing up and achieving independence from her mother. Nichols was born in Guyana in the Caribbean but moved to England when she was in her twenties. Possibly, then, the separation in the poem is a geographical one, i.e. Nichols moved abroad, but her mother didn't. Or perhaps the separation is more profound than either of these. Perhaps the past tense of the repeated phrase 'you were' indicates that the poem is, in fact, an elegy; the mother is in the past tense because she has died. This would make the celebration of the continuing positive influence of the mother, revealed in the tripartite of present participles, 'fathoming'; 'mantling'; 'streaming' more poignant.

The hybrid imagery in *Praise Song for my Mother* combines the universal with the culturally more specific. The first three metaphors compare the mother to aspects of nature essential to life everywhere, 'water', the 'moon' and the 'sunrise'. The mother was so important to her daughter that life without her could not be sustained, hence she was like water. The moon is a romantic image and the moon controls tides. The sun, of course is the source of light and warmth and 'sunrise' or dawn connotes new beginnings, new hope, fresh starts. In the final stanza Nichols shifts focus to more specific, more Caribbean images. Her mother is like a 'fishes red gill', like a tree's 'spread' and like delicious food. Again the emphasis is on the mother as a source of sustenance. The first two images are metaphors; Nichols' mother was like a fish's 'gills' again signals that she was key to life as fish breathe through their gills. 'Flame' obviously suggests power, passion and vibrancy, picking up the 'red' of the previous line, but the tree also offers protection. A 'spread' may also suggest abundance, like a buffet, as in the phrase a 'nice spread'. The final image contains associations the poet has about her mother, the preparation of food, the smell of cooking.

The reader doesn't have to work too hard to decode Nichols' imagery because mostly she uses conventional metaphors, symbols in fact, but also because in the last line of each of the first three stanzas she provides three explanatory adjectives. The extent to which this is necessary or effective is open to question. The influential modernist poet and critic T.S. Eliot developed the aesthetic of the 'objective correlative'. The role of the poet was to find the exact thing, a symbol, that could stand in for his or her feelings or ideas. Eliot believed it was redundant to explain this symbol, so for anger he might use 'the thunder', but he would not have written 'the thunder of his anger'. Nichols' adjectives provide us with some more information

 about each symbol: The mother was like water because she was 'deep' and understanding 'fathoming' [a pun on the measurement of depth], but also 'bold'. Now, we could argue that water does not possess either boldness or understanding and so the comparison of mother and water is a little loose. Similarly, 'pull' and 'grained' could be applied to both mother and moon, but 'mantling', in the sense suggested by CIE of 'cushioning, enveloping or surrounding' takes a bit more work. These ideas may pertain to the mother, but what does the moon envelope or surround? Surely the moon is surrounded by night. Perhaps the moon is cushioning because of its softer light. The adjectives applied to sunrise, 'rise', 'warm' and

'streaming' make sense, but the first, a repetition from 'sunrise', seems rather redundant. Would the poem be more effective, in fact, if a T.S. Eliot influenced editor had convinced Nichols to cut the third line in each of her first three stanzas? After the mild expletives, what might the poet have answered back to justify their inclusion?

Growth and change and separation

Perhaps we were being overly pedantic. These words don't just function as qualifiers for the symbols, they also contribute to the poem's form and its music. The form comprises three tercets followed by a five-line stanza, technically a cinquain, and then a single line on its own. The first three stanzas repeat the same pattern, with each line growing a little longer as the stanza develops. Clearly Nichols had a pattern of growth in mind here, reflecting the healthy, sustained growth of the child under her mother's care. The movement of the lines across the three stanzas, outwards and then back in, outwards and then back in, outwards and then back in, also generates a wave-like pattern, in harmony with the poem's imagery of moon and water and Caribbean heritage:

....
....
....

....
....
....

The last adjective in each three is also the longest, stretching out into a present participle. Moreover, it is active too, a verb as well as an adjective. Again a sense of growth is encoded into the poem, and there is something comforting, rhythmically soothing, about the 'x and y and z' pattern with the predictable 'ing' rhyme at the end of each stanza.

This regular pattern changes in the fourth stanza, signalling a change of course in the relationship between mother and child. There is a break - the form, the imagery, the pattern of imagery, change. But there is also continuity, expressed in the similar phrasing, 'you were...' and by the visually delayed, but then reassuring, reassuringly repeated, final adjective, 'replenishing'. Continuity and change are more prominent in this stanza, but have been implied in the poem from the start through the combination of present and past tense verbs. There is another change in the final stanza, comprising a single line, like the now solitary child. For the first time we also hear the voice of this beloved mother. For the first time an imperative is used, 'go', and the line is powerful because it shows the mother helping her daughter to achieve a better life with greater opportunities ['futures'] despite it entailing separating from her child. Letting go is one of the hardest things for parents to do, and, selflessly, this mother helps her child to part from her by commanding her to embrace a better future.

Nichols' poem does not end with a full stop. And that might make us notice, if we hadn't already, that there's no punctuation at all in the rest of the poem, no commas, question marks, hyphens, no full stops. Except one comma in the last line before 'you said'. <u>Why hasn't the poet used any standard punctuation?</u> <u>What is the effect, if any, of this choice?</u>

 If you're a teacher, perhaps you could present the poem first to a class without the name of the poet and with standardised punctuation. Without the poet's name, can the class guess whether the poet is male or female? What leads them to their conclusions? What can they determine about the poet's nationality and where they might come from? What sort of separation might the poem articulate?

'You were

water to me:

deep and bold and fathoming.'

Does that make any difference? Yes, I think it does. Punctuation separates out phrases, clauses, sentences. The lack of punctuation implies connection, continuity, freedom. There is no full stop at the end of the poem because the 'wide future' is before the poet; this is not the end of her story nor the end of her mother's influence. Unlike some other post-colonial writers, Nichols uses Standard English in her poem, she doesn't inflect English and write it phonetically, with a Caribbean accent, as her long-time partner, John Agard tends to do. Nichols does, however, use an African form, a praise song. Perhaps the lack of punctuation is a subtle rejection of the rules of Standard English. More importantly, however, the absence of punctuation in the rest of the poem makes that comma in the final line more significant. For a moment the mother's words are held in suspension, a small, pregnant pause conveys the emotion behind the mother's self-sacrifice, as well as her daughter's understanding and appreciation of this.

Praise Song for My Mother crunched:

YOU - WATER - DEEP - WERE - MOON'S - MANTLING - YOU - SUNRISE - WARM - WERE - GILL - SPREAD - PLAINTAIN - REPLENISHING - FUTURES

James K. Baxter, *Elegy for my Father's Father*

At one remove

James Baxter's unbroken, tower-like poem is a rather long lament for his grandfather. Rather than present his grandfather in a consistent light, or at a particular moment in his life, the poet constructs a composite and fragmented impression from different memories, perspectives and images. As the rather distant title signals - 'my father's father', rather than the warmer 'my grandfather' or warmer still 'my granddad'- the poem expresses ambivalent feelings about this figure and about his continuing influence on his family, including, of course, on the poet himself.

Though it's presented as a continuous whole, broadly the poem can be broken down into five distinct sections:

1. The first of these, starting with a slightly lyrical statement to the effect that the grandfather have never really expressed his feelings, 'his heart had never spoken', ends with a couple of metaphors that convey the power of the man's presence, but also dehumanise him.
2. The second section fast-forwards a little, taking us to the graveside and the mourners, mourning his death 'in their fashion'.

3. We then step back in time to the man the grandfather once was and learn of his physical vigour and strength.

4. The poem started an hour before the grandfather's death, moved forward to his funeral, then dropped back into a distant memory. In the fourth section, starting 'when he was old and blind', we enter the experience at another different moment, after the previous memory, but before the 'hour he died'. Noticing this might prompt us to consider why the poet chose this arrangement of time rather than ordering the events chronologically. We'll park that thought for the moment and return to it later [or perhaps earlier] in the essay.

5. In the last section we are back in the same moment and the exact same words the poem opened with, rather as if time has been suspended or circled back on itself in a loop. Embedded within this memory is another one, of a 'house by the waterside' taking us back, perhaps, to the grandfather's childhood.

Section #1

After a straightforward first few lines, Baxter shifts into more elevated poetic mode in the fourth line, opening with an emotive apostrophe 'O' and moving into metaphor. [Pedantically we might wonder perhaps how the poem's speaker knows what the grandfather felt in his last hour, especially considering his 'heart had never spoken'.] The metaphors appear to be of the grandfather, described first as a 'tall tower' and then as a 'cairn'. Both metaphors make him seem strong, but also stony and inhuman. But even if we decipher this, the phrasing and syntax make the meaning obscure. Is the meaning of lines four and five, for instance, that  unless the tower of his reticence is 'broken' no memorial for the grandfather will be allowed? Or is it that memorial is just 'denied' to the 'tall tower broken'? If so why? The colon indicates that the second metaphor further exemplifies the point. Okay, so, emotionally, the grandfather's like an 'unchanging cairn' [a stack of stones], though music could reach him, set him 'ablaze' and blossoming like a flower ['an aaronsrod'] which seems like an awkwardly mixed metaphor. The second image suggests that the tall tower did need to be broken down or set ablaze for proper memorial to take place.

Section #2

A snapshot of the funeral is delivered in just three lines. Is this the memorial that could have been 'denied'? The key detail is, of course, the reference to the grandfather's 'bitter veins' and how this infected blood flows into his descendants, including, presumably, the poet. That they mourn in 'their fashion' implies that not everyone felt great sadness at his death.

Section #3

Baxter's old-fashioned tendency to invert the normal word order is evident again in the descriptions of the physical prowess of the grandfather when he was a young man. The grandfather's strength and toughness are conveyed through his digging sods and carrying a tree on his 'shoulder', as if he were a giant. That he is able to do this under a hot punishing sun, the metaphorical 'lion sun', further strengthens the impression of this manly power and toughness.

Section #4

A stark contrast is established by describing the grandfather's physical incapacity, drunkenness and anguish. Sedentary and blind, he sits 'all day' by the fire. Once again, the poet's language takes off into metaphor. The adjective 'drunken' is transferred from the grandfather to the stars that, in his befuddled state seem to be 'dancing'. His mind has become destructive, a fiery 'burning-glass'. But, there is consolation. When he was sober he 'knew' the bleak 'winter world' is 'held in the 'hand' of the comforting 'green boughs of heaven', like a heavenly version of the world tree of the Norse myths. Characteristically, even this knowledge seems to lead, however, to uncommunicativeness: 'The pride of his heart was dumb'.

Section #5

We're back at the start, only now we have some amplification of the grandfather's terseness. He didn't speak 'his heart' in 'song' or even when he was in love - in the 'bridal bed'. Again, despite the lack of communication, the poet enters the grandfather's mind and takes us into his thoughts. This thought is 'naked' which suggests it is unguarded, vulnerable, true and it falls 'back', suggesting it happens without conscious control. On the other hand, an alternative reading could be that he deliberately 'falls back' on a memory for support. In either case, we deduce the mind is going back in time and the poem's narrative reaching for an origin, a revelation of why or how the grandfather became so emotionally repressed and taciturn. He remembers when nature seemed alive and in touch with his childhood self. Somehow the rather gothic, frightening image of the 'dark mouths of the dead' is comforting, because, unlike the grandfather 'the tongues of water spoke', and, moreover they spoke to him. In other words he felt in touch with nature to such an extent that even death was not frightening. Typically for a poem that is consistently ambiguous, the last line can be read in two radically different ways. Certainly it seems because he was in communion with nature, the grandfather was 'unafraid'. This could mean that when he was a child and had this connection at that time he was not afraid, in contrast to how he is now as an old, dying man. On the other hand, 'and his heart was unafraid' could refer to the comfort the memory of this communion with nature provides the grandfather in the hour before his death.

What are we to make us this peculiar poem? Its language veers from the ordinary and straightforward to the densely metaphorical. At times, inverting word order, sticking the verb at the ends of lines, it sounds like the poet's writing in the late Victorian period and is trying to sound like the Irish poet, W.B. Yeats. The poem starts off in rhyme, moves out of it, and comes inconsistently back into it at the end. There's a bit of Scottishness in there too, with the pipes and cairns. What is clear is that the poet had a difficult relationship with his grandfather. For an elegy, the poem presents a complex picture of this not entirely likeable man. Some of it is quite bleak and harsh. There is optimism, however, in the idea that within the grandfather's stony exterior a more sensitive soul was hidden. Being a poet might appear the ultimate expression of a sensitive soul, the starkest possible contrast between the two men. But the unsentimental view, tough words and unbroken tower of the poem's form suggest otherwise. Research the colourful, restless but short life of the New Zealand poet James K. Baxter and you'll find a man struggling to find his true identity.

Elegy for My Father's Father crunched:

[As this is a long poem, I'm going to pick words from most, but not every line]

DIED - NEVER - TOWER - DENIED - UNCHANGING - ABLAZE - THEY - BITTER - FASHION - CHAIN - TREE - SHOULDER - LION - BLIND - SAT - HOURS - DRUNKEN - BURNING - HEAVEN - WINTER - DUMB - DIED - SPOKEN - BRIDAL - NAKED - HOUSE - CHILD - AWAKE - DEAD - TONGUES - UNAFRAID

Charlotte Mew, *The Trees are Down*

Charlotte Mew's ecological poem is arranged on the page in an unusual, rather eccentric but also significant way. If you're teaching the poem, to foreground the form you could present it at first stripped of stanzas and lineation, i.e. as prose. As this is a long poem, pupils could work in small groups to re-arrange a section into the best possible shape. Everyone could have a go at the first section. Once the class have had as long as is productive, you could then reveal Mew's own formatting. Then they could have five or ten teacher minutes to work on another section.

Section 1:

They are cutting down the great plane-trees at the end of the gardens. For days there has been the grate of the saw, the swish of the branches as they fall, the crash of the trunks, the rustle of trodden leaves, with the 'Whoops' and the 'Whoas,' the loud common talk, the loud common laughs of the men, above it all. I remember one evening of a long past Spring turning in at a gate, getting out of a cart, and finding a large dead rat in the mud of the drive. I remember thinking: alive or dead, a rat was a god-forsaken thing, but at least, in May, that even a rat should be alive.

Section 2:

The week's work here is as good as done. There is just one bough on the roped bole, in the fine grey rain, green and high and lonely against the sky. (Down now!—) and but for that, if an old dead rat did once, for a moment, unmake the Spring, I might never have thought of him again.

Section 3:

It is not for a moment the Spring is unmade to-day; these were great trees, it was in them from root to stem: when the men with the 'Whoops' and the 'Whoas' have carted the whole of the whispering loveliness away half the Spring, for me, will have gone with them.

Section 4:

It is going now, and my heart has been struck with the hearts of the planes; half my life it has beat with these, in the sun, in the rains, in the March wind, the May breeze, in the great gales that came over to them across the roofs from the great seas. There was only a quiet rain when they were dying; they must have heard the sparrows flying, and the small creeping creatures in the earth where they were lying— but I, all day, I heard an angel crying: 'Hurt not the trees.'

My heart has been struck

Looking at how the poem is arranged on the page it's not hard to deduce the speaker's distress. The whole form looks rather erratic, unsettled and irregular. Scan down the left-hand side of the poem and you'll notice that lines start at different points, with some indented and others not. Scan down the ragged, jagged-looking right-hand side and you'll see how varied the line lengths are. The longest lines are very long indeed, having around fifteen or sixteen words [and even more syllables]; so long, in fact, that it's not quite clear where they end. Often when the poem's printed some of the words have to be moved down to a new line because they can't be fitted to the page. For example:

'With the 'Whoops' and the 'Whoas,' the loud common talk, the loud common laughs of the men, above it all.'

Should that count as one or two lines? In contrast, the shortest line is just two words and two syllables long. There's no metre either to keep the language in good, regular order. And all the irregularity is contained within stanzas that themselves are irregularly varied in length and size. There is a rhyme scheme but, of course, this too is irregular. The pattern established in the first stanza with the second and fourth lines rhyming, a xaxa pattern, has already changed to abab by the second stanza. By the third stanza the rhyme scheme has shifted again, to abccaddb, and then in the last stanza suddenly Mew uses couplets, including an insistent double couplet in the penultimate rhyme. If you're not totally convinced that the poem is constructed on a principle of shape-shifting irregularity, compare how it looks on the page with Larkin's poem, *The Trees*.

Now, we could argue that all this disorder and distress is as a result of the speaker's ecological sensibility. But the distress is so acute, the whole form of the poem so discombobulated that we might guess that there's rather more going on than this. Specifically we could conjecture that the destruction of the trees triggers memories of, or stands in for, other more poignant and personal losses in the poet's life.

Just one bough

The details of Charlotte Mew's biography are stark and tragic. The eldest child born into a middle class family in London in 1869, while she was still an infant three of Charlotte's brothers died. Later, another brother and then a sister were committed to mental hospitals where they would spend the rest of their lives. Her father's

premature death left the remaining family in a challenging financial position. Charlotte lived with her mother and sister, Anne, in rented accommodation. After their mother's death, the two surviving Mew sisters continued to live together. Because of the history of severe mental illness in their family, they decided never to marry so they wouldn't pass their illness on to children. After being forced out of their condemned home, Anne developed cancer and was nursed full time by Charlotte. After Anne's death, Charlotte slipped into depression, entered a nursing home for treatment, but committing suicide while there. As the Poetry Foundation says, 'The traumatic issues Mew grappled with during her childhood—death, mental illness, loneliness, and disillusionment—became themes in her poetry and stories.' [5]

So it seems, perhaps, that Mew has transferred her feelings of desolation and loss onto the trees. Behind the narrative of the trees lies the tragic story of her family.

Breaking apart, breaking down

In the first stanza Mew expresses the anguish she feels by using primarily sonic imagery. We hear the onomatopoeic 'grate of the saw', 'swish of the branches', 'crash of trunks', 'rustle' of leaves, as well as the shouts of the men. The men are anonymous and collective, a faceless 'they' who are causing this harm. No reason or explanation is given for their destruction of the trees. The sensitive speaker seems entirely isolated from these men whose comparative roughness is conveyed by repetition of the phrase 'loud common'. She seems plagued by their noisiness as much as by the destruction itself.

We have already highlighted the irregular quality of the poem, as evidenced through its line lengths, rhyme scheme, stanza form and so forth. Another example of this unsettledness is in the sudden break in the narrative at the  start of the second stanza. Here Mew begins a tangential recollection about how she found a 'dead rat' in her drive. This prompts her to reflect that May should be a time of new life, not death. Perhaps here there's an allusion to the scene from *King Lear* in which the old King asks despairingly 'why should a dog or horse or rat have life' and not his murdered daughter, Cordelia. If even a 'god-forsaken' rat should be alive, how much more so trees [and loved relations] that the poem's epigraph tells us we are ordered by God's 'loud voice' not to hurt.

Hurt not the trees

Though there isn't a new stanza, the poem then jolts us back into the present and the story of the destruction of the trees which has gone on apace. Quite suddenly there is only 'one bough' left and in a series of swift, bluntly truncated lines this

---

[5] From https://www.poetryfoundation.org/poems-and-poets/poets/detail/charlotte-mew

bough 'lonely against the sky' is 'down'. It doesn't take Sherlock Holmesian or Sigmund Freudian levels of genius to work out that Mew, the last surviving member of her family identifies herself with the personified bough. Hence the short, terse phrase and the exclamation mark. Why though is this gasp of horror in brackets and why the hyphen? Perhaps the punctuation conveys Mew's fear of the insignificance of her suffering to others. Her tragedy in the end was a private, isolated, personal one, suffered by her alone. And a hyphen is a punctuation mark whose function is to link things together. Here, poignantly, as in the Emily Dickinson poem, the hyphen links to nothing. Then we are back with the rat.

The 'old dead rat' changed Mew's perception, changed the spring atmosphere to something darker and colder. The destruction of the trees parallels the dead rat, only in this case, the damage is longer term. Whereas the rat's dead corpse casts a wintery chill over spring 'for a moment', the destruction of the trees is 'not for a moment'. 'Half the Spring' has been taken from the speaker when the 'great trees' with their 'whispering loveliness' have been removed. Again personification makes the experience seem more traumatic and personal and the adjective 'whispering' highlights the poet's communion with nature, almost as if the trees were her secret companions. It also emphasises through contrast her non-relationships with the

working men. The sense of communion is further underlined by the shared word in the phrase 'my **heart** has been struck with the **heart** of the planes' [i.e. plane trees]. Her life has been intimately connected with the trees, in tune and in rhythm with them through extremes. Once again, writing about her empathy for the trees Mew is surely writing about the tribulations and trials of her own life:

'The great gales that came over to them across the roofs from the great seas'

The adjective 'great' appears three times in quick succession. The trees and the gales and seas are all 'great' because to the poet there were momentous; they are the mysterious, elemental forces, larger than any individual and beyond their control, that shaped the drama of her life. All this greatness passes, poignantly, only with a 'quiet rain', as if hardly noticed, hardly lamented. Further personification, 'they were dying', 'they must have heard' expresses the poet's deep empathy, not only for the defenceless trees, but also for the 'small creeping creatures' with which she must have identified. Such suffering might be enough to make angels cry. At least there was some comfort for Mew in the fact that she could hear the angels, even if the rest of the world seemed as deaf as these common men to their heartfelt injunction.

The Trees are Down crunched:

THEY - GRATE - CRASH - LOUD - MEN - SPRING - RAT - GOD-FORSAKEN - EVEN - ONE - RAIN - HIGH - LONELY - DOWN - BUT - DEAD - UNMAKE - NOT - GREAT - WHISPERING - GONE - HEART - LIFE - WIND - GALES - DYING - SMALL - ANGEL - HURT

Philip Larkin, *The Trees*

A smart shirt and tie

Look at this poem on the page. <u>What impression does the form create?</u> <u>What adjectives would you use to describe it?</u> Comparing the form of *The Trees* with Charlotte Mew's poem, *The Trees are Down* helps to highlight each poem's distinct forms. Larkin's poem is neat, calm and orderly. Though it is quite slight, the poem looks well-constructed - solid and four-square. Three even, tidy looking quatrains are arranged in a regular pattern. Using the quatrain form, the poem looks traditional and conventional. Examine the form a little more closely and you'll see there's also a regular ABBA rhyme scheme, a form known as envelope rhyme. The rhymes are also all full and masculine. There's nothing about the form here that could be labelled avant-garde or experimental or outlandish. If the poem's form were clothing, it might be a tweed jacket, smart shirt and tie, perhaps some slacks or cords, finished off with a stout pair of brogues. Though, on reflection, 'stout' doesn't seem the right adjective for a short poem that, albeit rather obliquely, reveals a vulnerable sense of self.

Always at the edge of a crowd

Despite expressing some unpalatable views on a range of issues, most controversially on race, class and gender, Philip Larkin [1922-1985] was indisputably a great poet, certainly one of the foremost English poets of the second half of the twentieth century. Erudite and a critical success, Larkin was that rare beast, a poet who was also popular with a general readership who actually bought his books. The bookish, jazz-loving, unmarried, cycling academic librarian developed a gloomy Eeyorish public persona and many of his poems are infected with a profound bleakness. Famous examples include *This Be the Verse* which begins with an obscenity suggesting rather forcefully that parents can have a damaging effect on their children and ends with the magnificently miserable: 'Man passes on misery to man/ It deepens like a coastal shelf/ Get out as early as you can/ and don't have any kids yourself'! But in his best poems, tenderness and beauty counterbalance the temperamental depressiveness, and these qualities are so hard won, go so against the poet's natural grain, that they seem even more beautiful and precious and true. The same poet who wrote *This Be the Verse* also produced the final line, 'what survives of us is love' [though, characteristically, Larkin hedged this idealistic sentiment by saying this statement might prove 'almost true'].

The foremost member of The Movement poets who ruled the poetic roost throughout the 1950s and 60s in England, Larkin had a sharp, often satirical eye and as often a sharp, sardonic tongue. Like other Movement poets, his writing is characterised by its rejection of the avant-garde experimentalism of Modernism, by the skillful use of traditional English forms, by an ironic outsider stance, by its candour and by the poet's deployment of a mix of a slangy modern idiom with more elevated 'poetic' diction. Often it sounds in his poems as if the poet is simply speaking to us in his memorably pithy voice. It's a highly distinctive voice, one that is 'plain-speaking, sceptical, modest, unshowy, awkward, common-sensical'.[6]

This is not America

At the same time Larkin was writing poems like *The Trees* poets in America were developing the Confessional school. As you'll remember from our essay on *One Art*, Confessional poets put their own autobiographical experience front and centre of their work, writing with naked frankness about hitherto taboo topics such as sex, abuse and mental illness. These poets were 'letting it all out' in free verse forms that stuck two fingers up to the buttoned-up restraint of European verse. Larkin's poems can be read as the direct opposite of Confessional poetry. And yet, though the poet

---

[6] Hamilton & Noel-Todd, *Oxford Companion to Modern Poetry*, pp.325-338

directs our attention away from himself and doesn't use the first-person pronoun at all in his poem, we come to realise that writing about the trees allows him, indirectly to write about himself, his own feelings and, in particular his fear aging and of death. Although, having said that, the poem could just as well be about coping with some kind of trauma the speaker is finding it difficult to leave behind and move beyond.

Something almost being said

Tripping along a four-beat common metre, the declarative first line of the poem is very straightforward and unfancy:

'The trees are coming into leaf'

It doesn't seem, in fact, to be very poetic. It sounds rather like someone just talking. And that's exactly the point; this is poetry that is meant to be like overheard speech. The second line introduces a simile, but the language is again plain and ordinary. We many wonder how these two things are alike - it's obviously not a visual analogy, but the language doesn't draw attention to itself in any ostentatious sort of way. Really it is only when we arrive at the fourth line that we are presented with something more unfamiliar. New leaves and 'greenness', signaling the arrival of Spring, are conventional poetic symbol for new beginnings, new life, new hope. We may have felt we knew where the poem was going, lulled by its apparent conventionality and unhsowy style. However, Larkin delivers a little surprise in the last word, reversing the expected symbolism, so that now these hopeful things signify 'grief'. What sort of Eeyorish misery guts would do that, we might think. No, maybe that's a little harsh. Perhaps our curiosity will have been pricked and we want to know why this speaker views spring so gloomily.

The second stanza suggests that actually he isn't sure why he had this reaction. Opening with a question, the stanza continues to convey a speaking voice, one that is hesitant and uncertain, prepared to question itself. This poem isn't boldly declaring universal truths; rather the poet is taking us into the process of their thinking as they probe their own reactions. The speaker wonders whether it's envy that caused his grief. Personifying the trees, he contrasts how they are 'born again' whereas humans 'grow old'. Immediately he realises, however, this is just an appearance and that, in fact, trees grow old too, as shown by their rings.

Unresting castles

In a poem mostly composed of mundane language, albeit neatly arranged along tetrameters and finessed into rhyme, the metaphor in the last stanza sticks out and draws the reader's attention:

'...the unresting castles thresh'

It's a surprising metaphor for several reasons. First of all, a tree doesn't look much like a castle, so the metaphor doesn't really work visually. So, it must be the associations with castles - strength, security, stability, impregnability and so forth that Larkin wishes to connect semantically with trees. However, both 'unresting' and 'thresh' imply movement, in the latter case, violent movement. But castles cannot move. Imagine a castle threshing about. Exactly, you can't. Examine the wording of the rest of the line more carefully and you'll notice the adjective 'still', which can mean static as well as presently. Taking all these aspects together, pulling in different semantic directions, the image seems almost paradoxical. <u>So, is the image effective or not?</u> <u>What do you think?</u>

The trees might be growing older and yet they appear to be renewed each May in 'fullgrown thickness'. From this the poet draws a message that recalls the cliché about turning over a new leaf:

'Last year is dead, they seem to say,
Begin afresh, afresh, afresh'.

From this Larkin infers the lesson from the trees that he must put his worries about aging and death, or perhaps some trauma or bad experience, behind him and that he can begin again. Picking up the 'res' sound from 'unresting', the 'ess' from 'thickness' plus the 'res' and 'esh' sounds from 'thresh' 'sh', the repetition of 'afresh' finishes the poem with light, cleansing, liquidy sounds. Tripartite repetition is a rhetorical device, of course, so we get the impression that the poet is trying to convince himself as much as his reader that this hopeful message is true.

Perhaps that 'unresting castle' metaphor can be applied to Larkin himself and to his poetry and this poem, in particular. On the surface, Larkin might have appeared a fairly assured, grounded kind of chap. Well-educated, a successful author, a professional academic Librarian, smartly turned-out, sort of ordinary. As someone once called him, a nine-to-five chap who had found poetry. But underneath this solid appearance was a more sensitive, more complicated and more morbidly frightened self, always at the edge of a crowd, constantly 'unresting'. Larkin's poem, *The Trees*, has an ordinary title, uses ordinary language and looks pretty conventional on the page. A small castle, perhaps. However, indirectly, between its lines it conveys the speaker's fear and uncertainty and need for some sort of external reassurance that things can get better, that he will be able to carry on. Characteristically for Larkin, there is a reluctance to commit to absolutes. There's an indecisive hedging or unresting, born of an awareness of the unreliability of our perceptions and the partiality of our beliefs. The voice of the trees, for instance, is only 'like' 'something', and that 'something' is not actually said, but is 'almost' said, a very Larkin word. Similarly, the positive, affirming message the trees convey is hedged by 'they seem to say', hinting at the possibility that this could be a misreading, and, in fact, we're all doomed.

The Trees crunched:
LEAF - ALMOST - BUDS - GRIEF - BORN - OLD - TRICK - WRITTEN - CASTLES - FULLGROWN - SEEM - AFRESH

Siegfried Sassoon, *Attack*

There's ~~not~~ to reason why

If you've never heard of Sassoon you might expect a poem called *Attack* to be full of excitement and drama. Once you discover it's a war poem this might confirm your expectations. When, however, you learn that this is a WWI poem these expectations will probably radically change. Because war poetry before WWI often focused on heroism and the drama of battle, with the gusto of Tennyson's patriotic *The Charge of the Light Brigade* a famously thunderous example. WWI poetry, in contrast, particularly the poems written during the war, presented a very different version of the experience of conflict. Partly, of course, this was because WWI was a new and different type of war, a machine war with poison gas, machine guns, airplanes, tanks, high explosive shells, and because it was a machine war fought on a much larger scale than previous conflicts, across whole countries. It was an attritional war too, with armies dug deep into miles and miles of trenches facing each other through barbed wire and across the blasted landscapes of no-man's-land. Attack and counterattack. Trenches taken and taken back again. Then there was the mud, the lice, the rats, the relentless pounding of the big guns, the endless waiting and then the terror of going 'over-the-top'. And the poets of this war were the soldiers themselves, reporting from the front line, not trying to glamourise war, but debunking patriotic propaganda, determined to tell the ugly truths and convey the horrors and show the pity of war.

Known by his men as Mad Jack, Siegfried Sassoon [1886-1967] was a captain in the British Army. Sassoon was brave to the point of lunacy, once capturing a German trench single-handily [and then apparently sitting in it to read a book of poetry!]. His citation when he won the Military Cross said: 'For conspicuous gallantry during a raid on the enemy's trenches. He remained for 1½ hours under rifle and bomb fire collecting and bringing in our wounded. Owing to his courage and determination all the killed and wounded were brought in.'

However, as the war ground on and the deaths piled up, Sassoon became disillusioned and eventually embittered. What had originally seemed to him to be a justified war was turning into something different, prolonged not in a search for justice, but in a quest for victory and at whatever cost. So, bravely, he decided to make a stand. Sassoon threw his Military Cross into the Mersey River and wrote a letter to his commanding officer, entitled 'A Soldier's Declaration':

I am making this statement as an act of wilful defiance of military authority, because I believe that the war is being deliberately prolonged by those who have the power to end it.

I am a soldier, convinced that I am acting on behalf of soldiers. I believe that this war, upon which I entered as a war of defence and liberation, has now become a war of aggression and conquest. I believe that the purposes for which I and my fellow soldiers entered upon this war should have been so clearly stated as to have made it impossible to change them, and that, had this been done, the objects which actuated us would now be attainable by negotiation.

I have seen and endured the sufferings of the troops, and I can no longer be a party to prolong these sufferings for ends which I believe to be evil and unjust.

I am not protesting against the conduct of the war, but against the political errors and insecurities for which the fighting men are being sacrificed.

On behalf of those who are suffering now I make this protest against the deception which is being practiced on them; also I believe that I may help to destroy the callous complacence with which the majority of those at home regard the continuance of agonies which they do not share, and which they have not sufficient imagination to realize.

July, 1917.   S. Sassoon.

Sassoon's letter was published in The Times newspaper and read out in the House of Parliament. He could have faced a charge of treason and have been court-marshalled, but Sassoon was well-connected and influential friends convinced the authorities that he had gone temporarily insane as a result of his war experiences. Consequently he was sent to be treated for shell-shock at Criaiglockhart Hospital in Scotland where, fatefully, he would meet another poet, Wilfred Owen.

~~Charge~~ for the guns

Given this biographical context, it's less surprising that the experience of war presented in *Attack* is distinctly unheroic. It opens with 'dawn' a traditional motif from Romantic poetry. Conventionally dawn symbolises new life, new beginnings, new hope, as in the phrase 'dawn of a new age'. In Sassoon's poem these positive

connotations are soon dispelled through the adjectives 'massed' and 'dun'. The former is more normally used to describe an army, as in 'massed ranks' and rather than the vibrant light associated with dawn the colour is dull, browny-grey, like the colours of army uniforms. The light when it comes is alarmingly, violently unnatural, a 'wild purple' that reveals an ominous, hostile landscape of a 'menacing scarred slope'. Sassoon uses personification, describing the sun, a symbol of life and light, as 'glow'ring', as if burning and angry, the former picked up in 'smouldering'. The 'spouts' of 'smoke' continue the hissing sibilance of these opening lines and complete an image of a landscape that is a version of hell. Ominously the spouts 'shroud' the slope, hiding it from view, but also foreshadowing the deaths to come.

Unless we have the misfortune to come face-to-face with a real one, probably the idea of tanks doesn't seem too frightening to a modern reader. But we need to remember these machines were powerful new weapons in WWI. And Sassoon doesn't seem to know what to make of them. He describes their movement as if they are alive; moving stealthily, they 'creep'. But their awkwardness and clumsiness in the landscapes is also signalled by the fact that they 'topple' towards the 'wire', as if dangerously off balance. The poet then switches back to sonic imagery, describing the noise of battle as a 'barrage' that 'roars' like some sort of angry monster.

Starting with a wide angle, establishing shot, Sassoon composes the poem like a film. After the visual description of the landscape and then the eerily unnatural tanks the sound is turned up and then he switches to close-up shots of the men. The first words he uses establishes immediately that the men are not going to be presented as glorious heroes charging fearlessly into battle. Instead they are 'clumsily bowed'. And they are weighed down too, both literally and metaphorically, by a long list of the equipment that they have to carry.

~~The jaws of~~ hell

Unlike the seemingly gung-ho cavalry in Tennyson's poem, the movements of these men are not dynamic, they're not even orderly; they 'jostle', 'climb', 'leave' and 'meet' the terrible sounding 'bristling fire'. Both of these words resonate with earlier descriptions in the poem: 'Bristling' means spikily aggressive, so personifies the fire; fire can obviously mean gun-fire, but there also the sense that the 'smouldering' sun has now set the landscape ablaze. No wonder the men already look like ghosts with their faces unnaturally 'grey'. They are also dehumanised and de-individualised as 'masks of fear'. Their morale is low; no encouragements are swapped with each other, there is only 'muttering'.

In ironic contrast to the dehumanised men, Sassoon personifies two abstract ideas, time and hope. The former seems indifferent to the soldiers' fate; it is 'blank'. Time's indifference to the soldiers' suffering makes them seem more isolated, beyond help, outside of time. It also recalls the apparent indifference of the public back home and of some of the generals who sent 'glum heroes up the line to death' as Sassoon wrote elsewhere. Simultaneously, time is also 'busy' as the soldier's time is running out. Hope is embodied as an emblematic soldier. Rather than leading the way to victory, even hope cannot escape the dreadful mud and, as if ashamed, avoids eye contact. Sassoon finds a powerful way to express that there can be no hope now for these men.

Finally, as if the poet cannot bear it anymore and cannot help crying out in desperation, he breaks through the poem's composure and appeals directly to the reader, to the generals, to the public back home, and perhaps to God: 'O Jesus, make it stop!'

Up until this point, despite the terrible experience it describes Sassoon's poem had been composed. He appeared to be taking a third person perspective, as if he was observing rather than participating in the attack. Artistic distance is implicit in the re-arranging of this experience into pentameters and into a rhyme scheme. Focus on these aspects more intently, however, and you'll see that though each line has the requisite five beats of a pentameter, their distribution is erratic and irregular. Try to determine the poem's rhyme scheme and you'll notice how it changes and slips into and out of a regular pattern. In fact, with a pentameter and a rhyme scheme and thirteen lines *Attack* looks like a sonnet, an ironic form for a war poem. But if it is a sonnet, it's a broken, battered and incomplete one, one just about holding onto its shape. And, of course, it stops a line short of the full fourteen. As if the poet just could not go any further.

Attack crunched:

DAWN - GLOW'RING - SHROUD - MENACING - TANKS - BARRAGE - BATTLE-GEAR - MEET - FEAR - TRENCHES - TIME - HOPE - STOP

Boey Kim Cheng, *Reservist*

Boey Kim Cheng [1965 -] is a Singapore-born Australian poet of Chinese descent. In *Reservist* Kim Cheng ridicules the idea of national service in the military, an experience that is still compulsory for two years for young men in Singapore.

What would a government's ideal reserve army be like? A lean, mean fighting machine? Highly competent, professionally trained troops, fighting fit? Brave, committed, patriotic, intelligent, athletic young men and women, well equipped with state-of-the-art weaponry, ready and willing at any moment to support your standing army? If that's what you might hope for you'd be very disappointed with the reservists in this satirical poem, 'cos they're nothing like that.

A weary farce

Take our narrator. No, please do take him, as the old joke goes. And he is an old joke, too overweight, too world weary to be any use at all as a soldier. He expresses a distinct lack of enthusiasm for the exercises he has to undertake. And what century is he in? He's some sort of cod medieval knight and this is the twenty first century, is it not? Of course, the ridiculous medievalism is part of the poet's satire and has something in common with Monty Python's *The Holy Grail*. Even from the outset the narrator is already fed up with the whole sorry spectacle of national service, 'Time and again' he tells us, wearily. The allusion to Cervantes and *Don Quixote* indicates a cultured nature, but also underlines the foolishness and futility of this call-to-arms. The narrator really is not just making excuses, he's not fit to fight: his old bones are 'creaking'; he makes 'suppressed grunts' when he has to move; he has a comical pot belly which he has to tuck skilfully into his uniform. And it seems that he isn't the exception; the other knights are little better. The pronoun is 'we', the 'pot bellies' are plural. These men don't snap or spring to attention, they apologetically, pathetically 'creep'. The satirical tone comes to the fore again in the reference to the soldiers being 'betrothed' to the weapons whose sleekness only emphasises their not so sleek physiques.

Perhaps when the action starts things will get better and the old-stagers will come into their own, right? Wrong. Once the action starts things don't get any better, at all. The reservists are 'too old', 'too ill-fitted' to their task; they 'plod' heavily through forests. Again there is a sense of disillusionment and weary overfamiliarity with the whole foolish masquerade. Just as the weary and colourless adjective 'again' is repeated throughout the poem, here the equally colourless adjective 'same' is used repeatedly to convey disaffection and boredom - 'the same hills'; 'the same forests'; 'the same trails'; 'the same roar'. The narrator even calls the presumably military exercises 'tedious rituals'. He can't even rustle up any excitement, or fear, when faced with 'masked threats' and 'monsters', because he knows they are not real. Worse still, this experience infantilises the men, so that they are 'like children placed/ on carousels', going round and round, not getting anywhere, playing ridiculous parts in 'somebody's expensive fantasyland'.

The third stanza comes as a bit of a surprise then, to the soldier as much as the reader. Despite the elements of farce, it is still possible that these men might emerge as 'heroes', apparently. Eventually they will 'play the game' over and over again until it sends 'his lordship to sleep' with boredom. If you use something over and over again, sometimes, eventually it will wear out or break. So doing the same things over and over again they might just wear things down, 'march the same paths till they break'. And then, suddenly, 'new trails' will open up and awkwardly, 'stumbling' these men with arrive at freedom, the 'open sea', and the dawn of a new, better era, 'daybreak'. Hurrah!

With his hybrid sense of identity, Boey Kim Cheng writes about Singaporean culture as both an insider and outsider. Writing in the first-person, for instance, he imagines himself to be a reservist in the Singaporean army. However, he also takes an outsider view in the way that he ridicules and criticises compulsory military service. Although English is one of the languages of Singapore, Malay is the national language, so writing in English is also simultaneously inside and outside the culture. Finally, Kim Cheng's cultural references, such as the depiction of medieval knights and the allusions he makes in the poem to other works of literature and myth, such as to the Spanish writer Cervantes and to the classical Greek myth of Sisyphus, imply an essentially western framework of understanding.

Reservist crunched:
[As this is a long poem, we will have to apply a more forceful crunch]

AGAIN - IMPERATIVE - KING'S - COURT-MARTIAL - CREAKING – BATTLE - WEARY - CREEP - RUSTY - AGAIN - BETROTHED - CAVALIER - PLOD - SAME - AGAIN - CHILDREN - FANTASYLAND - TEDIOUS - SAME - SURPRISE - HEROES - HORRORS - SISYPHUS - GAME - LORDSHIP - BREAK - NEW - DAYBREAK

Wilfred Owen, *Anthem for Doomed Youth*

<u>What would you say was the single most remarkable thing about Owen's WWI poem?</u> His use of sonic devices to create the sound scape of battle, such as the 'the stuttering rifle's rapid rattle/ can patter out' which mimics the rat-a-tat-tat of machine gun fire? Or the extended conceit of the absence of funeral rites for these dead soldiers? Or, perhaps, that immediately striking, brutal first simile, for 'these who die as cattle'. Alternatively, you might suggest Owen's use of the sonnet form for a poem about war, but also about love. All of these are remarkable features, but, in my opinion the most remarkable thing about the poem is something absent from it, partisanship or animosity towards the enemy, the Germans.

The Hun

To fully appreciate how remarkable this absence is we have to wind the clock back and think ourselves into a young man's mind. An average young man, inspired to take up arms to defend his country, defend Europe, in fact, from German aggression. A young man who had swallowed all the propaganda he had been fed about the

Great War, how it was going to a terrific, once-in-a-lifetime adventure, how he was going to return a hero, how the war was going to be short and swift, how the enemy was some sort of ravening, brutish monster that had to be stopped. In particular the mother country and her women needed protecting from the German beast. Here's 'The Hun', depicted in American propaganda as a sort of giant King Kong type ape-monster making off with a semi-naked, helpless damsel. This image may be American, but British ones were just as bad. Demonizing your enemy, of course, is a common strategy in propaganda. Probably by the time the Great War had begun the average English Tommy had been brainwashed into thinking of the Germans soldiers as brutal, brainless monsters.

Inevitable corollaries to anti-German feeling at a time of war were nationalistic and jingoistic fervour about England and Englishness. Read, for example, Rupert Brooke's *The Soldier*, a celebratory hymn to England, to catch the flavour of these sentiments. Of course, as the title indicates patriotism is expressed in *Anthem for Doomed Youth*, except that the national boundaries of England and Germany have been replaced by a generational one, the 'doomed youth' of both nations. Owen's poem is as much a lament for young, dead German soldiers as it is for the young English dead. At a time of war, considering the context of virulent propaganda, this seems a remarkable triumph of empathy.

It's an odd sort of anthem. Think of national anthems for a moment. Imagine you are a committee choosing a new one for a new country. What are you looking for? What are the key attributes of a successful national anthem? That it should be uplifting, stir the soul, have a feeling of grandeur and an impressive scale. That it should celebrate the unique identity of the country and its history. Think of *Land of Hope and Glory*. Last night of the proms. Owen's poem certainly isn't rousing. It's a dirge or a lament, a song for the dead. Owen's choice of the word 'anthem' is, then, bitterly ironic.

What passing-bells

As we mentioned at the start of this essay, Owen's poem is constructed around an extended metaphor, technically known as a conceit, comparing the soldiers' deaths on the battlefield with the rituals of a funeral: Rather than having 'passing-bells' the men are led away to be brutally and casually slaughtered, like 'cattle'; instead of last prayers [orisons] for their eternal souls, they have the pounding of artillery and the rattle of rifle fire; instead of mourners and a choir they have wailing shells and bugles. In the second stanza, the sonnet's sestet, instead of candles, the only 'holy glimmers' they will see are in each other's eyes before death comes; rather than a funeral pall over their coffin they will have only the pale faces of their loved ones left behind in England and in lieu of flowers they will have only these women's tenderness. Finally, instead of having the blinds drawn as a sign of mourning, these men will face a greater darkness, that of eternal night falling. The implication is that not only are these men being led to slaughter, but that their sacrifice is not even adequately acknowledged or mourned for, let alone honoured. Perhaps even their chance of an afterlife is being denied. By whom? By the army, perhaps, and also by a population back home who had little idea of the true horrors - the gas attacks, going over the top, the barbed wire, the dead and dying in no-man's-land, the rats, the lice, the endless mud, the dead bodies, the ceaseless pounding of the big guns, the closeness of death, the blasted landscapes - of prolonged trench warfare. Like his friend and fellow war poet, Siegfried Sassoon, Owen wanted to puncture the complacency of the civilian population and try to get over to them the realities, truth and pity of the Great War.

So, perhaps, rather than the Germans, the real enemies were the callousness of the Generals sending men to be butchered and the indifference of the civilian population and the politicians who continued the war. Certainly Sassoon thought so and he famously said so in a letter published in The Times newspaper. Sassoon would have faced the severest of military discipline if his friends had not managed to plead he was suffering from temporary insanity and ship him off to Craiglockhart hospital in Scotland where he would meet Owen for the first time. But there's another enemy in this poem and it appears in many of Owen's WWI poems.

Machine war

Sometimes in Owen's poems it can appear that nature and perhaps even God have either abandoned or worse actively turned against the soldiers. But a more persistent threat is the technology of warfare. WWI was the first 'machine war'. Though machine guns had been used previously, in the Boer War for instance, the ones used in WWI were far more efficient and far deadlier. Added to this was the new horror of gas shells and towards the end of the war, tanks and fighter planes. In *Anthem for Doomed Youth* Owen uses personification in a bitterly ironic way. It seems that as the men are dying helplessly the machines are taking on a life and a will of their own. It is almost as if the weaponry is acting of its own accord, following its own mad logic without any human influence. There is a monster  here, but it's not the German army; Owen describes the sound of the big guns [English and German] as 'monstrous anger'. He also uses the adjective 'stuttering' to describe rifle fire. This word suggests the intermittentness of the firing, but also implies that the rifles might jam. More importantly, it is as if the weapons are speaking - they 'patter out' the men's prayers. 'Patter out', of course, can mean 'make the sound of', but also implies cancelling out, erasing. The shells are also personified, as a choir of 'shrill, demented' voices, 'wailing'. The madness and anger and monstrosity of the war seems to emanate from the technology and the soldiers are helpless before it.

Noticeably the imagery in the first stanza is predominantly aural. We hear the discordant din of battle, the anger, the stuttering, the wailing, guns, rifles, shells, bugles. The imagery of the second stanza is more visual and the tone more elegiac. In particular, Owen uses the symbolism of light, specifically light going out in references to candles, eyes, glimmers, pallor and finally dusk falling.

Owen's poem has to stand in for the absent mourning and funeral rites for the dead soldiers. He offers his own lament as a way of honouring these inescapably 'doomed youth'. They were doomed because they faced impossible, insurmountable odds. Yet Owen when he was invalided to Craiglockhart with shellshock and could have sat out the rest of the war, chose to go back and fight alongside his men. Owen had the choice to sit out the rest of the war, but, knowing the full horror of the experience he chose to go back. Why? Because he was a captain in the British army and he could not bear the thought of abandoning his men. It was a decision, of course, that cost him his life at the tender age of just 25. Not only in his poetry then, but with his life, Owen demonstrated his deep respect, compassion and sense of honour for his fellow soldiers, German as well as English.

Anthem for Doomed Youth crunched:

CATTLE - MONSTROUS - RATTLE - PATTER - PRAYERS - CHOIRS - DEMENTED - BUGLES - SPEED - EYES - GOOD-BYES - PALL - TENDERNESS - DUSK

Hone Tuware, *Friend*

Soapbox oratory

Hone Tuware [1922-2008] was a celebrated New Zealand poet of Maori ancestry. From a working-class background, at one time a card-carrying communist, Tuware was associated throughout his life with various tribal and left-wing political movements. Such political affiliations are evident in his poem *Friend*. For instance there is an ecological and spiritual element in the close relationship the poem articulates between the speaker and the wild, natural New Zealand landscape. In addition, there is a pervasive sense of the richness that can be discovered and enjoyed by everyone, the 'jewelled fantasies' despite monetary poverty, as evidenced by the poet's 'rags'. Moreover, these 'rags' are labelled paradoxically as 'splendid', suggesting the poet is, in some ways, proud of the poverty of his childhood. Finally, there is an implication that the land, and the freedom the poet once had to roam in it, has now been lost, either to ecological decay or perhaps commercial development.

Jewelled fantasies

Addressed to someone with whom the poet shared the adventures of childhood, *Friend* presents a rich, sensual description of their experiences and the landscape that sustained them and fired their imaginations. Immediately the setting tells us that the children were free to play far from civilisation and the control of adults. It was a 'wild stretch of land' near to the sea with a 'lone tree', a symbol of the place's isolation. There they did typically childish, perhaps boyish, things, such as building a 'fort' and engaging in pretend warfare so that the 'air was thick with the whirr' of spears. The specifics of a natural New Zealand landscape and its flora mix with universal aspects of childhood adventures. The spears, for example, are made from the exotic-sounding 'toetoe', a type of grass native to New Zealand. The food too is exotic, 'oyster-studded roots' and 'eels' from a 'mangrove' swamp. The relish of cooking what you yourself have caught is, however, universal.

Visual imagery of the 'stretch of land' and the 'lone tree' combines with sonic imagery, of the 'sharp-tongued sea' and the 'whirr' of spears that makes the air

tangible, 'thick'. There appear to be two voices in the poem too, harmonious voices, with the description of the 'feast' in italics, as if spoken by the friend. As there will be later in the poem, with the description of 'splendid rags' and 'jewelled fantasies' here the poet emphasises the richness they found in poverty. The roots are 'studded' with oysters, a verb associated with diamonds; the eels are like precious metal, 'silver-bellied', the tree's leaves are 'fine-edged' and create a delicate 'silken tracery' on the contrastingly 'cracked clay floor' and the superlative feast, 'no finer', was 'cooked' in only a humble, basic 'rusty can'.

Now, however, this brightly-lit, dreamtime world of childhood and its remote landscape has gone, it is in the past. The tree from which they built the fort is 'dead wood now' and the sound of play battle has been replaced by 'the grey gull's wheel'. The tree they 'climbed', that provided 'food and drink' to their imaginations 'is no more'. The 'shared days' have 'broken ends', which may suggest some sort of falling out that needs to be repaired. Hence, while celebrating their shared childhood experiences, Tuware's poem is also a lament for what has been lost.

The jewelled past has gone. The present, in stark contrast, the poet tells us is 'drear' and 'dreamless'; the world has become 'hurt' and 'troubled'. In part, no doubt this is due to the change from an innocent childish perception to a more experienced adult one. As we grow older inevitably we become aware of the complexities and challenges of life. But there is also a clear sense that the world too has changed for the worse. Nature has suffered, the tree has died. In this troubling context the poet reaches out for the sort of companionship he enjoyed as a child. In the modern world, he now feels weaker and more vulnerable and needs 'reassurance'. If they can share nothing else they can at least share their jewelled memories. The final stanza expresses a wish that seems rather forlorn: 'Perhaps the tree/ will strike fresh roots again'. If it is dead the tree it won't be able to develop new roots, whatever the plaintive poet might wish.

The local and the universal

As we have said, some elements of Tuware's poem are particular to New Zealand, others are almost universal. The most obvious examples are the poem's imagery and depiction of the relish of childhood adventure, freedom and self-sufficiency. The poem depicts an innocent world of childhood, within a sustaining natural landscape, recalling the work of the English Romantic poets, such as Blake, Coleridge and Wordsworth. Like those poets, Tuware contrasts this small, rich world with a more troubled, wider one of adult experience. The form of Tuware's poem also sits within and outside the conventions of the European poetic tradition. For instance, the poet uses quatrains and conventional poetic images, but, on the other hand he doesn't use metre or end-rhyme. The poem's form also changes in an irregular, unconventional manner. After the stability of the first three stanzas, describing the secure world of childhood, the poem's form becomes less dependable and predictable, only returning to the reassuring quatrain in the final stanza. And, of course, the poem is written in English, not in Polynesian. Often when post-colonial writers use English they subvert it or impress their own indigenous culture upon it, by, for example, including native words or deviating from standard spelling and syntax. Tuware uses absolutely Standard English. All these factors combine to articulate Tuware's sense of universal experience, the value of friendship and finding richness in experiences in tune with nature, experience that cannot be bought, or sold, by money.

Friend crunched:

REMEMBER - WILD - LONE - SEA - FORT - DEAD - WHIRR - SUCCUMBS - STUDDED - FEAST - SILVER - RUSTY - BROKEN - SHARED - WANTED - TREE - FOOD - MORE - FINE-EDGED - WHISTLE - SILKEN - CLAY - FRIEND - DREAR - DREAMLESS - REASSURANCE - FANTASIES - RAGS - PERHAPS - FRESH - SHADE - TROUBLED

Emily Brontë, *Cold in the Earth*

At the edge of the grave

One distinctive feature of Emily Brontë's stoical, lyrical poem is the use of oxymoronic phrasing. For example, in the fifth stanza the poet writes of 'sterner desires' and 'darker hopes' and in the last stanza she refers to 'rapturous pain' as well as to 'divinest anguish'. A similar pattern can be discerned in some of the rhyming too, particularly in the sixth stanza where 'perished' is rhymed with 'cherished' and 'destroy' sonically bolted together with 'joy'. What is the significance of this pattern? Well, as it does in Tennyson's poem, it suggests that the poet was pulled violently in opposite directions at the same time and that her feelings were deeply ambivalent. The central issues the poem wrestles with are how to deal with terrible trauma and yet keep going in life; how to strike a balance between honouring the past and living in the present; how to remember without losing oneself to memory. Brontë's speaker wishes to remain faithful to her dead beloved and is emotionally drawn to remembering their precious love. But this source of happiness is simultaneously also the source of terrible sadness, and thinking too much of her dead love might tempt the speaker to give in to despair and collapse into her own grave.

Ellis Bell

A few words about Emily Brontë's life: The author of the Gothic Romance *Wuthering Heights*, Emily Brontë [1818-1848] was one of an extraordinary creative group of siblings. Both her sisters, Charlotte and Anne, became famous novelists and her brother, Branwell was an artist. Brought up together in a parsonage in the small town of Howarth in West Yorkshire, the Brontë children created an imaginary world, Gondal, about which they wrote stories. Relatively little is known about Emily's life. She appears, it seems, to have been a reclusive figure, shy and withdrawn, but with a great love and empathy for nature, the moors in particular, and all its creatures. Though she was sensitive, she must also have been robust and determined. Life in Howarth in the first half of the nineteenth century could be harsh, especially perhaps for sensitive young women. One way to escape was through writing and these three young women hoped to have their writing published. But to be published, the Brontë sisters had to adopt male names, with Emily becoming Ellis Bell.

Emily died at the age of only thirty. One grim contributory factor to her ill-health was the fact that the water supply to the parsonage where she lived her whole, short life was contaminated from run-off from the nearby graveyard. A suitably Gothic detail for a poem about still being in love with someone long dead.

Sweet Love of Youth

We learn that the anonymous addressee of the poem died some time ago, fifteen years ago, in fact, half Emily's lifetime, and the ardent, empathetic speaker feels guilty that they have not kept his memory always fresh in their mind. The dead lover is 'far, far removed' in that he is under the cold earth, but also far distant in time. Nevertheless, despite all the 'change and suffering' of the intervening years, the narrator has remained absolutely faithful: 'No other sun has lighted' her life. This man or woman was her 'Only Love'. Brontë powerfully conveys the shadow this death threw over her, or her speaker's, life. [We cannot be sure that the poem is autobiographical or whether Brontë's novelistic imagination has created this archetypal lost-love scenario. Indeed, some versions of the poem are titled differently and appears, that, initially at least this was a Gondal poem. To observe this distinction between writer and poetic persona for efficiency's sake we'll refer to the speaker or narrator of the poem.] The mirroring lines of stanza five contrast a happy before with a terrible after:

'All my life's bliss from thy dear life was given -
All my life's bliss is in the grave with thee'

That simple word 'all' conveys the speaker's devastation. Stoically, they had to discover a way of surviving the loss of all happiness. Even though she has gone past even the power of 'Despair' to destroy her, she finds a way to keep going. It is almost as if the pressure splits her into two selves; the heart or 'young soul' that continues to weep 'tears of useless passion' and the head that, like a school teacher or priest, 'sternly' tells the heart/soul these tears serve no purpose, are 'useless'.

As we've said, the poem tells an archetypal story of lost love. What makes Brontë's version more memorable than numerous others in a similar vein? For one thing, Brontë avoids the danger of writing something self-indulgent, self-pitying, morbid or mawkish: 'woe is me, look at how I suffer' sort of thing. The combination of the passionate, animated voice of the narrator, the vividness of the figurative language and the resilience this speaker shows, embodied in the poem's form and structure, make this poem remarkable. Powerful emotions are expressed powerfully, but are also held in check, kept at bay by the counterbalancing forces of reason and the will. In short the poem is admirable for both its artistic virtuosity and for the strengths of character it articulates.

Faithful indeed

From the opening line the poem's speaker shows imaginative empathy. Rather than

express her own misery and suffering, the speaker feels pity for her dead lover as if he or she still suffers in the grave. For instance, she imagines the coldness they must suffer, the weight of the 'deep snow' piled above them and the dark dreariness of the grave. She also sternly criticises herself, measuring her own behaviour harshly by the most exacting of standards. Despite her faithfulness and loyalty she worries that she has fallen short somehow and that this is a form of betrayal of her lover's memory. Her own suffering remains in the background, only sketched in. 'Darker hopes' for example, 'beset' her like enemies, but we don't learn what these actually are. She avoids the pitfalls of self-pity.

Moreover the speaker demonstrates great fortitude. Despite the terrible strength of her emotions she does not cave in to them. Despite the fact that the light and bliss has been struck out from her life and her 'golden dreams' have 'perished' she teaches herself to exist and, extraordinarily, even to 'cherish' an existence 'strengthened and fed without the aid of joy'. This is a tough, stoical soul indeed. How many of us could bear, let alone cherish, a life without any joy in it? It is an iron will that is able to 'check' her own feelings and to 'wean' herself, like a mother weans a baby. The speaker is almost torn in two by her contrary desires. She externalises her own 'soul' as an 'it' with an ardent 'burning wish' to destroy itself, but 'sternly denied' this release by the other half of herself. The balance to be struck between remembering and forgetting is an impossibly delicate and fine one. It is as if the speaker is on a tightrope; if she forgets too much she will lambast herself and feel she has betrayed her love and so topple into an abyss; if she remembers too much, indulges in the 'rapturous pain' she will also topple into the abyss. Or, perhaps, she's standing at the edge of a cliff, the tempting oblivion below her. She could take a step forward or back. Hence she repeats that she 'dare not' remember too much. In either metaphor, she is in dire peril, and it takes all her strength to resist the easier option.

The World's tide

Several memorable figurative images animate the poem. For example, the speaker feels cut off from their dead beloved and memories of them and Brontë expresses this viscerally, writing that they have been 'severed' by 'Time's all-wearing wave'. Here the verb conveys the agony of separation, while the time as a wave metaphor conveys the helplessness of a lone individual in the face of huge,  elemental forces that 'wear' her resistance down. This image is picked up and amplified later in the poem when the speaker refers to the even larger force of the 'World's tide' bearing her helplessly along, like some piece of flotsam.

Brontë also imagines her thoughts to be like a bird, hovering over a landscape and 'resting their wings' by the lover's grave. The dream of flight is a dream of freedom, of course, but how much more potent such a dream must have been for a woman so confined by nineteenth century society, a woman who lived reclusively in the same house all her life. Only in her imagination could Emily take flight like this, in her novel and in her poetry.

Predominantly Brontë's imagery is drawn from nature and from nature's most powerful, elemental forces. As well waves and sea, birds and flight, the speaker refers to her lover as light bringers, her 'sun' and her 'star'. Emotions within her are so strong that they almost feel like physical objects, the 'divinest anguish' of memory she imagines as being like a drink, of wine or poison, that could obliterate the 'empty world'.

It's not just the imagery that makes the poem visceral and vivid, however. We have already mentioned the use of paradoxical phrasing, but there are other distinct patterns, such as the capitalisation of important words and repetition. The capitalised words are the principle players in the drama, the central characters in the narrative: The 'Only Love', 'Time', 'World', 'Sun', 'Star', 'Despair', 'Memory'. Words and sometimes phrases are repeated, often quite closely together. For example, 'cold', 'far', 'ever', 'cold in the earth', 'hopes', 'no other', 'all my', 'bliss' and 'dare'. Obviously repetition can be used for emphasis, but it also seems at times that the speaker has to say words twice as if to really believe and accept their meaning. Such a distinct, insistent pattern of twoness inevitably makes us think of the two lovers and of the tension between the two forces on which the poem and the speaker are strung, remembering and forgetting, love and loss.

The will in action

Strong emotions may have triggered the poem, but as strong a will shaped and mastered these feelings into the ordered, composed and accomplished form the poem takes. Eight orderly and even stanzas with a consistent, alternating rhyme scheme are powered by a slightly thickened pentameter. Full rhymes click into place with clockwork-like precision. Only once does the poet deviate from the regular pattern, in the first stanza, when, poignantly she rhymes 'thee' with 'thee', as if that word dominates her mind and erases alternatives. Brontë has taken raw emotional experience and fashioned it into a ringing bell. This is the triumph of art over grief, but it is also an act of commemoration for her lost love.

Cold in the Earth crunched:

COLD - GRAVE - FORGOT - SEVERED - ALONE - MOUNTAINS - WINGS - NOBLE - FIFTEEN - MELTED - FAITHFUL - SUFFERING - LOVE - BEARING - BESET - WRONG - HEAVEN - OTHER - BLISS - GRAVE - GOLDEN - DESPAIR - LEARN - STRENGTHENED - CHECK - SOUL - BURNING - TOMB - DARE - MEMORY - ANGUISH - EMPTY

NB

Of course, Emily Brontë's most famous depiction of an intense, doomed love was in her novel *Wuthering Heights*. If you liked her poem, perhaps you might want to real this extraordinary, passionate and haunting book with its infamous, star-crossed lovers, Catherine and Heathcliff, depicted below in the 1939 film version.

Robert Browning, *Meeting at Night*

Browning's poem lends itself well to a re-ordering activity. Presenting it first to a class without a title and the lines out of sequence will help them identify key clues to the narrative structure and highlight the virtuoso rhyme scheme. With an able class you could give them the whole poem, or, alternatively have them work just on the first stanza, and then show them this before they work on the second. Give them around ten teacher minutes to work on the poem, perhaps in pairs. After five minutes reveal the first line and maybe ask which the most effective last line would be. Once they've sequenced the poem correctly, give them a couple of minutes more to put it into stanzas. It could, for instance, be arranged into six couplets, four tercets, three quatrains...Whatever arrangement they choose ask them to justify this in relation to what the poem appears to be about. Finally, ask them to come up with a suitable title. Come back to this after you're gone through and analysed the poem, giving pupils a chance to revise their title.

Poem x
Three fields to cross till a farm appears
The grey sea and the long black land;
In fiery ringlets from their sleep,
Than the two hearts beating each to each!
As I gain the cove with pushing prow,
Then a mile of warm sea-scented beach;
; A tap at the pane, the quick sharp scratch
And the startled little waves that leap

And blue spurt of a lighted match,
And the yellow half-moon large and low;
And a voice less loud, thro' its joys and fears,
And quench its speed i' the slushy sand.

A few bold strokes

The poem's narrative is told swiftly and economically in a series of bold, almost filmic images. Each line of the poem adds a new layer to the story. Visual imagery is predominant. We see 'the grey sea', 'the long black land' and the 'yellow' moon. These details are the equivalent of establishing shots in films; sketching in place and time, they are also all in-between two states - the moon is incomplete, 'half'; we are between sea and land, and between night and day. [We'll return to the significance of this in-betweeness later in this essay.]

Personification of the waves which are 'startled' by the boat's oars conveys the general hush and secrecy. Presumably the speaker is travelling in the dangerous half-light, while the sea and the land are 'asleep', to avoid being discovered. 'Fiery ringlets' captures the play of yellowy moonlight on the waves, but the poet also chose this phrase because we associate 'ringlets' with hair, and particularly women's hair. In this way Browning hints at the nature of the story, a clandestine meeting of lovers, a tryst, and generates anticipation by hinting at future events. Subtly, he also takes us into the excited mind of the male lover, so preoccupied with his beloved that he sees her image mirrored everywhere in the world around him.

Speedily we arrive at a 'cove', a perfect place to arrive undetected. The sensory, visual imagery is now supplemented here by a combination of figurative, aural and tactile images. For example, Browning use the verb 'quench' to describe the boat entering the beach. Again, there's a number of good reasons for choosing this contextually surprising word: Firstly its sonic qualities combine with the line's sibilance and its last 'ch' sound echoes the 'sh' of 'slushy', so that a mimetic effect is generated. Secondly, 'quench' is a verb usually associated with thirst; it means to sate an appetite. Heat too can be said to be quenched. So, again, the male lover's desire, to quench his own appetites, is projected onto the world around him, conveyed through the way he perceives his experiences. Olfactory imagery is soon used, so almost the full range of possible sensory imagery is used to take us into the scene. The beach is 'warm' [tactile] and 'sea-scented'.

In one line a mile has been travelled as if the action of the poem is accelerating. We cross three fields in a heartbeat and we're suddenly at the farm. Here Browning

switches momentarily back to auditory channel only, turning off the visual entirely. Why? Because this creates a moment of suspense. Notice too how, like a film director, Browning uses very quiet, small sounds to draws us further and closer into the tense hush. Why doesn't the narrator just bang on the front door? For that matter why has he come cloaked by the night? We infer that someone else in the house would not welcome his visit. Will his lover be there for him or will he be caught and have to face the consequences? Hence the quiet 'tap at the pane' - his signal to her. Then the 'quick sharp scratch' of a match and we're still not sure until he hears her voice, even quieter than the scrapey the match, despite her heightened feelings of 'joys and fears'. These daring lovers are defying prohibition. Like Romeo breaking into the Capulet garden in Shakespeare's play, the narrator enters the farm.

The final line of the poem is a classic image of intimacy and mutuality - 'two hearts' beating in time with each other, as if beating to each other. Finally the distance between them has been traversed and they are as close, physically and emotionally, as it is possible to be. They may fear discovery, but the lovers are reunited and have each other. In that moment, romantically, nothing else seems to matter.

Double double

The last line of the poem mentions '**two** hearts' that are beating '**each** to **each**'.

That's two things, twice, a pair in a sentence, and also a sentence itself split into two. The poem also has two stanzas that mirror each other. Tenuous connection? Coincidence? What about:

1. The grey sea and 2. the land
1. the yellow and 2. half moon
1. The yellow-half moon and 2. large and low
1. Large and 2. low?

Still not convinced? Check through this short, intense poem and you'll find that not only do most lines fall into two natural halves, but the adjectives frequently appear in pairs too. Examples of the former: 'A tap at the pane' and 'the quick sharp scratch' or 'in fiery ringlets' and 'from their sleep'. Examples of the latter:

- 'long, black'   'yellow half'
- 'startled little'   'warm sea-scented'
- 'quick, short   'less loud'

The virtuoso rhyme scheme also pairs words, and through sound enacts a coming closer together and a moving apart, with two rhymes meeting in the middle of each stanza like lovers. So, in summary, twoness is encoded into the weft and weave of the poem, into the stanza form, into the rhyme scheme, into the syntax and into the imagery. It's even there in a title in which the first word can be read either as a verb or noun. This twoness emblematises the lovers and unites them, counterbalancing forces of in-betweenness in the poem that hold them apart. In the end, the magnetic force of attraction is the strongest in the poem.

Coded language?

Meeting at Night is a Victorian poem and notoriously the Victorians were very prudish about sex. Sex was a taboo topic for polite conversation and for literature. Even if they were minded to, Victorian writers also could not write directly about sex because their work was subject to strict censorship. The result was that when Victorian writers wrote about sexual relations they wrote about them through coded, symbolic language. Now, modern students can also be a little prudish about sex and embarrassed about discovering sexual imagery in poetry, even shocked to find it in canonical poems from the olden days set by examination boards for them to study. And there is a danger that once you start looking for phallic imagery you tend to find it everywhere. Nevertheless, even with this warming in mind, there does appear to be an erotic dimension to Browning's poem. For example, the description of the boat, with its 'pushing prow' entering the cove. Perhaps too the blue spurt of the lighted match. Enough already? Okay, we'll draw a modest veil over this topic.[7]

Two hearts beating each to each

Although Browning's poem may well be a work of pure fiction, a little biographical information about his relationship with his wife, the poet Elizabeth Barrett Browning, might suggest otherwise. Not least due to Robert's relative poverty, Elizabeth's family and her father, in particular, did not approve of their relationship and tried to dissuade Robert from courting his daughter. Despite her family's hostility, Robert

and Elizabeth were determined to marry and secretly eloped in order to do so. After their marriage, the couple lived abroad, in Italy, making their way in the world despite the fact that Elizabeth's father disinherited her as a result of the marriage. Though *Meeting at Night* might not describe a real, biographical experience, it must surely be informed by Robert's relationship with Elizabeth and the struggles they went through.

The poem is Victorian, so it's not surprising that the dynamic agency in *Meeting at Night* is male. It is the man who travels over the perilous sea, in darkness. It is the man who must cross the fields and arrive at the forbidden farm. Discovery for him would probably have more dire consequences than for his beloved who does nothing more than wait for him and respond to his tapping. This presentation of courtship

---

[7] Less squeamish readers might be interested in Tom Paulin's essay in *The Secret Life of Poems*, in which he really goes to town on the erotic suggestiveness in Browning's poem, waxing lyrical, for instance, on the rhyming: 'the paired rhyme words 'beach' and 'each' [are] like the soft smack of kisses'.

may be typically Victorian, but it also reflects the biographical reality that it was Robert who seems to have done most of the running in his courtship of Elizabeth.

Meeting at Night crunched:

GREY - HALF-MOON - STARTLED - RINGLETS - COVE - QUENCH - MILE - FARM - SCRATCH - SPURT - VOICE - EACH

'Poetry is only there to frame the silence. There is silence between each verse and silence at the end.'

ALICE OSWALD

A sonnet of revision activities

1. Reverse millionaire: 10,000 points if students can guess the poem just from one word from it. You can vary the difficulty as much as you like. For example, 'quench' might be fairly easily identifiable as from Browning's poem whereas 'match' would be more difficult. 1000 points if students can name the poem from a single phrase or image – 'portion out the stars and dates'. 100 points for a single line. 10 points for recognising the poem from a stanza. Play individually or in teams.

2. Research the poet. Find one sentence about them that you think sheds light on their poem in the anthology. Compare with your classmates. Or find a couple more lines or a stanza by a poet and see if others can recognise the writer from their lines.

3. Write a cento based on one or more of the poems. A cento is a poem constructed from lines from other poems. Difficult, creative, but also fun, perhaps.

4. Read 3 or 4 other poems by one of the poets. Write a pastiche. See if classmates can recognise the poet you're imitating.

5. Write the introduction for a critical guide on the poems aimed at next year's yr. 10 class.

6. Use the poet Glynn Maxwell's typology of poems to arrange the poems into different groups. In his excellent book, *On Poetry*, Maxwell suggests poems have four dominant aspects, which he calls solar, lunar, musical and visual. A solar poem hits home, is immediately striking. A lunar poem, by contrast, is more mysterious and might not give up its meanings so easily. Ideally a lunar poem will haunt your imagination. Written mainly for the ear, a musical poem focuses on the sounds of language, rather than the meanings. Think of Lewis Carroll's *Jabberwocky*. A visual poem is self-conscious about how it looks to

the eye. Concrete poems are the ultimate visual poems. According to Maxwell, the very best poems are strong in each dimension. Try applying this test to each poem. Which ones come out on top?

7. Maxwell also recommends conceptualising the context in which the words of the poem are created or spoken. Which poems would suit being read around a camp fire? Which would be better declaimed from the top of a tall building? Which might you imagine on a stage? Which ones are more like conversation overheard? Which are the easiest and which the most difficult to place?

8. Mr Maxwell is a fund of interesting ideas. He suggests all poems dramatise a battle between the forces of whiteness and blackness, nothingness and somethingness, sound and silence, life and death. In each poem, what is the dynamic between whiteness and blackness? Which appears to have the upper hand?

9. Still thinking in terms of evaluation, consider the winnowing effect of time. Which of the modern poems do you think might be still read in 20, a 100 or 200 years? Why?

10. Give yourself only the first and last line of one of the poems. Without peeking at the original, try to fill in the middle. Easy level: write in prose. Expert level: attempt verse.

11. According to Russian Formalist critics, poetry performs a 'controlled explosion on ordinary language'. What evidence can you find in this selection of controlled linguistic detonations?

12. A famous musician once said that though he wasn't the best at playing all the notes, nobody played the silences better. In Japanese garden water features the sound of a water drop is designed to make us notice the silence around it. Try reading one of the poems in the light of these comments, focusing on the use of white space, caesuras, punctuation – all the devices that create the silence on which the noise of the poem rests.

13. In *Notes on the Art of Poetry*, Dylan Thomas wrote that 'the best craftsmanship always leaves holes and gaps in the works of the poem so that something that is not in the poem can creep, crawl, flash or thunder in'. Examine a poem in the light of this comment, looking for its holes and gaps. If you discover these, what 'creeps', 'crawls' or 'flashes' in to fill them?

14. Different types of poems conceive the purpose of poetry differently. Broadly speaking Augustan poets of the eighteenth century aimed to impress their readers with the wit of their ideas and the elegance of the expression. In contrast, Romantic poets wished to move their readers' hearts. Characteristically Victorian poets aimed to teach the readers some kind of moral principle or example. Self-involved, avant-garde Modernists weren't overly bothered about finding, never mind pleasing, a general audience. What impact do the CIE anthology poems seek to have? Do they aim to amuse, appeal to the heart, teach us something? Are they like soliloquies – the overheard inner workings of thinking – or more like speeches or mini-plays? Try placing each poem somewhere on the following continuums. Then create a few continuums of your own. As ever, comparison with your classmates will prove illuminating.

Emotional..intellectual

Feelings..ideas

Internal..external

Contemplative..rhetorical

Open...guarded

Terminology task

The following is a list of poetry terminology and short definitions of the terms. Unfortunately, cruel, malicious individuals [i.e. us] have scrambled them up. Your task is to unscramble the list, matching each term to the correct definition. Good luck!

Term	Definition
Imagery	Vowel rhyme, e.g. 'bat' and 'lag'
Metre	An implicit comparison in which one thing is said to be
Rhythm	another
Simile	Description in poetry
Metaphor	A conventional metaphor, such as a 'dove' for peace
Symbol	A metrical foot comprising an unstressed followed by a
Iambic	stressed beat
Pentameter	A line with five beats
Enjambment	Description in poetry using metaphor, simile or
Caesura	personification
Dramatic monologue	A repeated pattern of ordered sound
Figurative imagery	An explicit comparison of two things, using 'like' or 'as'
Onomatopoeia	Words, or combinations of words, whose sounds mimic
Lyric	their meaning
Adjective	Words in a line starting with the same letter or sound
Alliteration	A strong break in a line, usually signalled by punctuation
Ballad	A regular pattern of beats in each line
Sonnet	A narrative poem with an alternating four and three beat
Assonance	line
Sensory imagery	A word that describes a noun
Quatrain	A 14-line poem following several possible rhyme schemes
Diction	When a sentence steps over the end of a line and
Personification	continues into the next line or stanza
	Description that uses the senses
	A four-line stanza
	Inanimate objects given human characteristics
	A poem written in the voice of a character
	A poem written in the first person, focusing on the emotional experience of the narrator
	A term to describe the vocabulary used in a poem.

GLOSSARY

ALLITERATION – the repetition of consonants at the start of neighbouring words in a line

ANAPAEST - a three beat pattern of syllables, unstress, unstress, stress. E.g. 'on the moon', 'to the coast', 'anapaest'

ANTITHESIS - the use of balanced opposites

APOSTROPHE – a figure of speech addressing a person, object or idea

ASSONANCE – vowel rhyme, e.g. sod and block

BLANK VERSE – unrhymed lines of iambic pentameter

BLAZON – a male lover describing the parts of his beloved

CADENCE – the rise of fall of sounds in a line of poetry

CAESURA – a distinct break in a poetic line, usually marked by punctuation

COMPLAINT – a type of love poem concerned with loss and mourning

CONCEIT – an extended metaphor

CONSONANCE – rhyme based on consonants only, e.g. book and back

COUPLET – a two-line stanza, conventionally rhyming

DACTYL – the reverse pattern to the anapaest; stress, unstress, unstress. E.g. 'Strong as a'

DRAMATIC MONOLOGUE – a poem written in the voice of a distinct character

ELEGY – a poem in mourning for someone dead

END-RHYME – rhyming words at the end of a line

END-STOPPED – the opposite of enjambment; i.e. when the sentence and the poetic line stop at the same point

ENJAMBMENT – where sentences run over the end of lines and stanzas

FIGURATIVE LANGUAGE – language that is not literal, but employs figures of speech, such as metaphor, simile and personification

FEMININE RHYME – a rhyme that ends with an unstressed syllable or unstressed syllables.

FREE VERSE – poetry without metre or a regular, set form

GOTHIC – a style of literature characterised by psychological horror, dark deeds and uncanny events

HEROIC COUPLETS – pairs of rhymed lines in iambic pentameter

HYPERBOLE – extreme exaggeration

IAMBIC – a metrical pattern of a weak followed by a strong stress, ti-TUM, like a heart beat

IMAGERY – the umbrella term for description in poetry. Sensory imagery refers to descriptions that appeal to sight, sound and so forth; figurative imagery refers to the use of devices such as metaphor, simile and personification

JUXTAPOSITION – two things placed together to create a strong contrast

LYRIC – an emotional, personal poem usually with a first-person speaker

MASCULINE RHYME – an end rhyme on a strong syllable

METAPHOR – an implicit comparison in which one thing is said to be another

METAPHYSICAL – a type of poetry characterised by wit and extended metaphors

METRE – the regular pattern organising sound and rhythm in a poem

MOTIF – a repeated image or pattern of language, often carrying thematic significance

OCTET OR OCTAVE – the opening eight lines of a sonnet

ONOMATOPOEIA – bang, crash, wallop

PENTAMETER – a poetic line consisting of five beats

PERSONIFICATION – giving human characteristics to inanimate things

PLOSIVE – a type of alliteration using 'p' and 'b' sounds

QUATRAIN – a four-line stanza

REFRAIN – a line or lines repeated like a chorus

ROMANTIC – A type of poetry characterised by a love of nature, by strong emotion and heightened tone

SESTET – the last six lines in a sonnet

SIMILE – an explicit comparison of two different things

SONNET – a form of poetry with fourteen lines and a variety of possible set rhyme patterns

SPONDEE – two strong stresses together in a line of poetry

STANZA – the technical name for a verse

SYMBOL – something that stands in for something else. Often a concrete representation of an idea.

SYNTAX – the word order in a sentence. doesn't Without sense English syntax make. Syntax is crucial to sense: For example, though it uses all the same words, 'the man eats the fish' is not the same as 'the fish eats the man'

TERCET – a three-line stanza

TETRAMETER – a line of poetry consisting of four beats

TROCHEE – the opposite of an iamb; stress, unstress, strong, weak.

VILLANELLE – a complex interlocking verse form in which lines are recycled

VOLTA – the 'turn' in a sonnet from the octave to the sestet

Recommended reading

Atherton, C. & Green, A. Teaching English Literature 16-19. NATE, 2013

Bate, J. Ted Hughes, The Unauthorised Life. William Collins, 2016

Bowen et al. The Art of Poetry, vol.1-14. Peripeteia Press, 2015-17

Brinton, I. Contemporary Poetry. CUP, 2009

Eagleton, T. How to Read a Poem. Wiley & Sons, 2006

Fry, S. The Ode Less Travelled. Arrow, 2007

Hamilton, I. & Noel-Todd, J. Oxford Companion to Modern Poetry, OUP, 2014

Herbert, W. & Hollis, M. Strong Words. Bloodaxe, 2000

Howarth, P. The Cambridge Introduction to Modernist Poetry. CUP, 2012

Hurley, M. & O'Neill, M. Poetic Form, An Introduction. CUP, 2012

Meally, M. & Bowen, N. The Art of Writing English Literature Essays, Peripeteia Press, 2014

Maxwell, G. On Poetry. Oberon Masters, 2012

Padel, R. 52 Ways of Looking at a Poem. Vintage, 2004

Padel, R. The Poem and the Journey. Vintage, 2008

Paulin, T. The Secret Life of Poems. Faber & Faber, 2011

Schmidt, M. Lives of the Poets, Orion, 1998

Wolosky, S. The Art of Poetry: How to Read a Poem. OUP, 2008.

About the author

Head of English and freelance writer, Neil Bowen has a Masters Degree in Literature & Education from Cambridge University and is a member of Ofqual's experts panel for English. He is the author of *The Art of Writing English Essays for GCSE*, co-author of *The Art of Writing English Essays for A-level and Beyond* and of *The Art of Poetry*, volumes 1-14. Neil runs the peripeteia project, bridging the gap between A-level and degree level English courses: www.peripeteia.webs.com.

The Art of Marking

The art of marking's pretty hard to master
knowing just what and what not to write,
like writing poetry, only somewhat harder.

Gather all the enthusiasm you can muster
clear your mind, concentrate your might,
for the art of marking's pretty hard to master.

Sharpen those pencils, straighten the page, and after
adjust the chair, change the angle of the light.
(It's like writing poetry, only somewhat harder).

Avoid a backlog building up, you'll only feel aghaster -
piles of books haunting your dreams at night -
the art of marking's pretty hard to master.

Top tip; better not to mark books when plastered,
Those witty comments? Best keep them out of sight,
like writing poetry. It's far more harder

to concentrate, when swinging from the rafters,
so, settle down, quietly your mind to the task apply.
The art of marking's pretty hard to master -
Like writing poetry, only somewhat harder.